JULes
on
SCHOOLS

JULES
on
SCHOOLS

Teaching, Learning, and
Everything in Between

JULIA M. WILLIAMS, PH.D.

Clover Valley Press, LLC
Duluth, Minnesota

Clover Valley Press, LLC
6286 Homestead Rd.
Duluth, MN 55804-9621
USA

The author and publisher wish to thank Robert Boone,
publisher of the *Reader Weekly,* for generously allowing the
inclusion of columns in this book that were originally printed in
biweekly column format in his publication.

Cover and interior design by Sally Rauschenfels
Cover photograph by Julia Cheng

Printed in the United States of America on acid-free paper.

Library of Congress Control Number: 2007942790

ISBN 10: 0-9794883-2-X
ISBN-13: 978-0-9794883-2-0

Acknowledgments

MY ACKNOWLEDGMENTS COULD EASILY and essentially include all of those whose lives touch mine. Without them all, I would have nothing to which to react, no meaning in context, and no one to validate or inspire my observations.

Therefore, my acknowledgments first include all of those teachers, administrators, parents, colleagues, and schoolchildren whose everyday interactions speak volumes about teaching and learning and what comes between.

Taking this collection of individual entries and bringing them together has been a magical process, due to the skill, bravery, and outstanding gifts of my publisher, Charlene Brown. She is supportive, exacting, encouraging, and definitive in the same sentences, and she is why this is a book. I cannot give her enough thanks, ever.

Our development consultant, LeAne Rutherford, has been priceless in this process. She is a treasure at the University of Minnesota Duluth, and she provided such fine eyes for structure and statements, with wonderful smiles and enthusiasm as well.

My colleague, Dr. Helen Mongan-Rallis, is an outstanding professor, and she so deserves credit or blame for several direct interventions in my life as a teacher, including the connection of my work with my publisher.

I would also like to thank Hobart, for his heart, and for his faith and belief in me.

Finally, I would like to thank these children, who are here in these pages, and who are and have been my reason to work, write, learn, and live:

Rachael,
Steven,
Celeste,
Justine,
Mitchell, and
Skylar.

This book is dedicated to my mother,
Norma June Hellickson Snelling,
and to all of my teachers.

Contents

Preface

BEING A PARENT OF SCHOOLCHILDREN, a teacher of schoolchildren, a school administrator, or a taxpayer supporting schoolchildren is to be part of a baffling yet beckoning world of promise and disappointment. Trying to make sense of our system of education, which is so important to each child, to the future of communities, and to the people who work within its confines, is daunting and complex.

To be able to see that system through more than one lens is helpful. To see it through several lenses simultaneously provides a viewpoint that allows for parents, students, teachers, community members, administrators, and policy makers to share common understandings with common language.

For the past three years, the biweekly column "Jules on Schools," carried by the *Reader Weekly,* published in Duluth, Minnesota, has attempted to provide multiple perspectives on education in our region. The columnist, Julia M. Williams, brings a lifetime and career as a mother, stepmother, high school teacher, Minnesota State Department of Education specialist, licensed principal and superintendent, staff developer, and professor of future educators to her writing and to her thinking.

Her essays have been posted in teachers' workrooms, read to staff at faculty meetings, quoted in commencement addresses, and cited by school board members across the northeastern portion of Minnesota. Collecting the columns and offering them here to readers as a themed, annotated collection provides many points of view at once, on issues and ideas, contemporary and timeless, that affect parents, children, teachers, and administrators.

The columns were written in response to the author's experiences, the time of year, the activities of her children, events in school politics, and ultimately in response to the way that life happens. The writing balances her personal life experiences with the life of schools and schoolchildren.

The two worlds are never entirely separate. Reflections on schools and schoolchildren should be grounded in heartfelt experience, educational theory, as well as on perceptive analysis of the forces that influence our world of education. Collected in this volume, these columns provide a unique and considered framework that brings many points of view together and sheds a different light on what happens in schools today.

A Welcome from the Author

WHEN BOB BOONE, publisher of the *Reader Weekly*, first approached me to write for his paper, he told me that he wanted to publish a Family/Education column, written by someone with a family who was also involved in education.

I have a family. I am mom and stepmom to six children, and I love each one of them dearly. My children have come to me by being born of my own labor and from that of two other women whom I now consider to be good friends. I am rarely sure of the combination that will gather together at my home at any one time, and that doesn't make my life simple.

I also have a career in education. As for my preparation for this career, I hold an undergraduate degree in English Education, a master's degree in Curriculum and Instruction, a Secondary Principal's license, a Minnesota District Superintendent's license, and a Ph.D. in Educational Leadership. I am blessed by being able to be a faculty member in the College of Education at the University of Minnesota Duluth (UMD). I have the immense good fortune of instructing both pre-service, master's, and now doctoral-level educators. I get to see the huge, energized hope and clear focus of the candidates for degree, and I see the strong and purposeful dedication of those who have spent real time in the field. I also have had the privilege of working with administrators and with teachers in designing staff development and in creating strategic plans.

I know that learning is an instinct. Teaching is a calling. Parenting, of course, is a blessing beyond measure.

In my current position at UMD, and in my former position as a regional coordinator for the Minnesota Educational Effectiveness Program, I have never met a teacher or an administrator who was not determined to do the right thing for kids. Never. Agreeing on what that right thing is…well, that's the really hard part.

I know that learning is an instinct. Teaching is a calling. Parenting, of course, is a blessing beyond measure. Our capacity to love is infinite, but our capacity to understand is somewhat limited. I also know that there are no simple, perky, one-size-fits-all answers.

Every morning there are people who wake up at my house and get ready to go to school. Some go happily to learn and teach. Some go to play the sports or to see their friends. Some go because they have to, or because their ride is waiting. Each one of them began kindergarten full to bursting with excitement and potential. For some, school has been fabulous. For others, it has been more difficult. We are on the home stretch now. Most of the children have graduated from high school, four are in college, and one is in graduate school. I have seen a lot of ups and downs and have a lot of stories, but none of this process of preparing effective individuals for tomorrow has been simple.

Perhaps it is because of the complexity of our world that the voice from one who tries to navigate chaos is a voice that is reflective of our real situation. A lot of us out here have been humbled by both intended and unintended consequences—enough so that we are not sure of a true path to perfect schools and perfect children.

In this book, I have examined some of the real issues we face as educators and parents, and I have attempted to share with you some of the wonders we are learning about how we learn and how schools and parents can use what we are learning. I highlight some of the ways things are working for kids and illuminate some of the things we need to study further.

I don't know who said it, but I love the phrase, "In chaos, there is opportunity." Perhaps because our world is changing so fast, because we spend so much time in confusion, and perhaps because, especially as parents and educators, we cannot take a break and just catch up, we need to connect. We need to learn and grow and go forward in our roles, holding hands, and reaching out to embrace the opportunity that surrounds us and the children we love. We parents, teachers, administrators, and students probably need each other more than we even know.

—Julia M. Williams

I. TEACHING

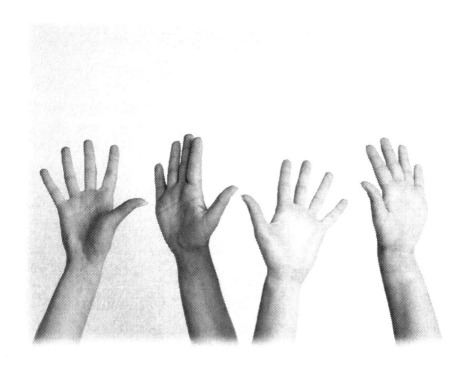

WHAT JOY AND WHAT RESPONSIBILITY we assume when we decide to teach. I think I always knew that I would be a teacher. My mother was a teacher, in a time when few of my friends had mothers who worked outside of the home. My mom taught English in Hutchinson, Minnesota. She went back to work when I was in the fourth grade, and I remember how privileged I felt when she let me correct spelling tests. I was so proud of my mother. She wore her hair in a French roll, and she dressed in skirts and nylons, every day.

As a very young girl, I set up desks in our basement and taught my younger sister and brother...something, probably. I set up a library over my bed, using envelopes cut in half to hold checkout cards for neighbors who wanted to read really good books—like Nancy Drew and Trixie Belden and all. I fell asleep, night after night, with my pillow in the closet (the door shut to cover the light), with a book.

During the holiday breaks, sometimes mom would let me help her check her students' *A Christmas Carol* projects. I read a lot of one-page biographies on Charles Dickens. I was afraid of Marley's ghost.

I tried to be other things. I wanted a journalism major in college, but I couldn't type fast enough. I considered law, seriously. My father counseled against it because he thought it would be depressing. I now have two lawyer brothers, however. I loved literature, and writing, and so I decided to try to teach. It was the best thing I ever did.

I am at home and at peace when I am with learners. I feel effusively alive when I am faced with the challenge of creating new understanding in the minds of students. There is nothing as gratifying, as twinkling and elusive, as that flash of new knowing. Achieving that is what I live to do. I think it is what I was born to do.

I take my profession seriously. If I wish to provide new ways of seeing the world to my students, I must constantly study. I must know what is out there to teach in my field. Then I must find ways to help students make their own sense of that information.

I am not alone, by any long shot. Teachers are like that. They are.

Since I am writing this for publication, I am hopeful that this page will stand as notice to my children, or to whoever may bury these bones some day.

I wish my stone to read MOTHER and TEACHER. That's all. Those are the words that define my life and make me proud of my life.

Falls, Leaps, and Atomic Theory

....

Every year, they begin as strangers and then become so very important.

ALL THE SIGNS ARE HERE, the flashes of red amid the dulling green, the aura of yellow lurking over the woods, the droop of the spring stalks, and the end of the endless evenings. My children are registering for courses. I am mostly writing checks. Every so often, I spy a wandering school bus, and because I am a person who defines herself as a teacher, fall is never just a season. There have been times in my life when I have not been employed by schools. During those years, fall was difficult. The sight of the school bus on the first days of school, the clean new backpacks, the making of the paper-bag book covers, the idea that students were filing into classrooms and I wasn't there to greet any of them was painful.

I find myself spotting for freshmen as I drive into the university campus these days. I am excited to see the new students, and I am anxious to see the returning students, too. It feels wrong to be in a building, to work in my office, where the sound of young voices engaged in energetic debate is absent. The lack of students doesn't just leave silence. It creates a vacuum, and we all know that nature abhors a vacuum.

So, as I wait and listen for them to come, I cannot help but wonder who they will be this semester. I am old, so I kind of know who I will be, but they do not yet have themselves pegged and pinned. I work with students who are learning to become teachers, and I have watched candidate after candidate begin to define who they will be when they greet their own first classes. I am consistently awestruck by the snowflake nature, the infinite variation, apparent in those who will someday teach school. I am inspired by their capacity to watch others teach and to filter those practices they will adopt from those that do not fit their personalities.

I am so grateful that those who are learning to teach are exposed to many different styles of teaching. I am also grateful for the fact that our schools are designed to allow for the individual natures of the wide array of gifts educators can bring to their classrooms. I am so glad that my students and my own children have learned from those teachers who think like they think. I am even more glad that my students and my children have had to learn how to understand those teachers who think differently, value differently, and act differently.

There are, of course, archetypical teachers, the ones we see in movies and on television and sometimes in real life. According to Edward Pajak in his book *Honoring Diverse Teaching Styles: A Guide for Supervisors* (2003), one could look at teachers categorically through almost a Jungian lens and classify them into four categories. I find his categories fascinating.

Pajak names his categories "knowing teachers, caring teachers, inventing teachers, and inspiring teachers." It's kind of fun to remember who taught me and what categories I have had represented in my education. Pajak identifies "knowing teachers" as being efficient, getting results, having standards and procedures in place, and emphasizing facts. I remember my high school chemistry teacher as being just such a fellow. Except, I did stay late one day, just to ask him about atoms. I asked him what would happen if we were wrong about the atom. We had never seen one. What if everything we based on atomic theory was fairy dust and as mythical as Hercules? He putzed about for a while and then gently told me that we can only understand as far as we are able, and that currently the structure of the atom made sense in application, but the theory of its actual nature was, like all science, an attempt to explain more than we can understand. It was then that I began to appreciate the passion behind his procedures and the faith beneath the formulas.

Pajak describes the "inventing teacher" as one who is focused on the future, on possibilities, on ideas. He believes that such teachers constantly test hypotheses and solve problems based on concepts and that they are aware of the big picture. I saw such a teacher when I rented the movie *School of Rock,* I think. They are the teachers who become excited by a new insight, a new interpretation—they are always discovering. I had one in ninth grade for English. *The Iliad* was new to him every year because he taught us to see it through the eyes of our current situations. How exciting!

"Caring teachers," according to Pajak, are the ones who nurture and who place the content of the course far below the people enrolled in it. These teachers are guided by the desire for harmony, and they work hard to provide a supportive classroom climate. These are the ones who have faith in you when no one does. These are the teachers whose hearts are so big that they push their brains right out of their ears sometimes. These are the teachers we run to for shelter.

The final category includes the "inspiring teachers," the ones who liberate through learning, who can paint the world in all its infinite glory and possibility. These teachers are empowering and cannot abide students who act with no underlying values. These are the ones who challenge and challenge and challenge until you cannot help but grow. These are the Robin Williamses in *Dead Poets Society*.

So, fall after fall we greet one another, not knowing what kind of combination our gatherings will bring. We don't know the potential of the linkages among students or between students and teachers, but in the fall, the air is electric with the sparks of possibilities. We don't know if we will enter situations in which we, or our children, will be cared for, inspired, invented, or imparted. We don't know what will be unlocked, overlooked, or which ambitions will take fire or wither. We truly face the unknown each year. We, being students and teachers, bravely and respectfully stand at the edge of the cliff each fall. Then, we all take a deep breath and a leap of faith and begin.

Ready, Bright, and Shining

···

Back to school is what fall has been all about for years to many of us.
For some, it is a sad ending, but for others, it is a chance to begin again,
a clean slate with no mistakes.

EVEN WITH GLOBAL WARMING AND ALL, it sits heavy in the air. It feels like we've turned a corner, or come over the top of a hill, because now we can see it, and whether it is as big as the gate of an ancient cathedral, or small as Alice's rabbit hole, the phenomenon is undeniable. If we are still, we can even hear the creak and groans as schoolhouse doors everywhere open wide, and everyone, inside and outside, gets ready for the entrance.

I watched, on Sunday morning, from a boat tied to the dock on Madeline Island, as island children waited for the ferry, their cars packed full with pillows, pots and pans, and the hearts of parents. University of Wisconsin students had already heard the creaking of college doors this weekend and were heeding the call from wherever they summered, even on that island. The co-eds jumped out of the cars in line to hug one another, their moms and dads, and the girl selling tickets to cross over. The ferry loaded, and the dads put their arms around the moms, and they turned to walk back to an uneasy peace on a front porch somewhere in the middle of Lake Superior.

It's not like we don't know that it's coming. It happens every year. For retailers, I swear it starts in June. We have all watched the stores morph from garden-and-patio to back-to-school, which will be most likely followed by Christmas on about September 5. We see the omnipresent erasers and chalkboards, apples, and wide-lined paper pictured on displays and on signs in store windows, although I am not sure that chalkboards and chalk and erasers are even used in many classrooms anymore.

For those of us with kids in college, we find ourselves spending disproportionate amounts of time filling out forms, over and over again, and searching for extra-long sheets and the bag of dirty clothes that disappeared in May. For those of us with kids in schools everywhere, we are receiving "Welcome Back" letters, and lists of what our children need to succeed in their grade this year, item by item. Our children begin each peer conversation with "Who'd you get?" Then the big question follows, "What are you going to wear?"

As parents, we find ourselves wondering how we are going to pay for any of it, from tuition to leggings. We all want to give our children what it will take to even the field. We all want them to walk in proud, not cowed and ashamed. We do what we can.

We feel the shift from ebullient pastel florals worn by tanned teens to the subdued hues of faded jeans and jackets carried "just in case." We see the ads for this year's backpacks and graphing calculators. If we work in schools, we know that these days are usurped by meetings and schedules and hectic, urgent preparations, and we know that the football teams are practicing in earnest, driven to be faster, stronger, and more powerful than the sum of their parts. At this time each year, the boys and their coaches know that it is yet possible to win them all.

Because it is. Now, before it begins, it is yet possible for every team, and indeed for every student, to live a year of triumph without failure. It is still possible that each entering student will be welcomed to a year of success after success in every way, and that each student will return to summer faster, stronger, happier, and more powerful than they stand this fall.

Our experience, of course, has told us differently. Our experience has taught us that our schools will hurt some children. We will harm, alienate, and lose a certain percentage by spring. We will not succeed with every child. We never have.

But, right now, when the tomatoes are magnificent, and we are glimpsing the blush on green apples, ubiquitous success feels possible. It feels possible that we can keep them all, that learning together in schools can live up to its promised joy and contribution. It feels possible that we can see, unlock, and nurture the champions that rest beneath the tanned skin of each child who enters the doors.

What a marvelous event this "back to school" is! It is a magical time of pure potential, pure promise, and possibilities. It is indeed a time to be savored and admired, for it will flash by quickly, as always.

We will awaken tomorrow with the backpacks on clearance, and the certain knowledge of colder days ahead.

Stitches

··

*As teachers, we soon learn that what students see is far beyond
what we teach overtly. We, most likely, will never know what place
we occupy in the lives of our students.*

I HAVE ONLY RECENTLY LEARNED THAT such things are called
"singularities." I have always known that they were something.

We all have had them, the singular moments that we knew were something, when our understanding changed. I know I had a lot of them in
school. I know a lot of them were provided by teachers.

I remember one, starting at a point when my forehead bashed into the
uptake lever of a sewing machine in ninth grade. I am old, so this class
happened back in a time when all
girls were required to take Home
Economics, and I had somehow
managed to sew my long, long
hair, stitch by stitch, down the
seam of a double-knit polyester
dress, and I had become trapped in
the machine and the garment, and
it hurt.

*Singularities happen
when you teach school.
As a teacher, you will
never know how many
you provided. You rarely
see them coming.*

My teacher's name was Elaine
Ensign. Ms. Ensign calmly walked over to me, grabbed a seam ripper,
released my head from the machine, and then painstakingly started, stitch
by stitch, to free me from the polyester. As she worked her way up the
seam, she dismissed one class, took attendance for the next one, talked
through the making of a mousse, admonished the girl who fed the last
mousse to her boyfriend in the hall, noticed the yellow in the eyes of
another girl, and sent her to the nurse to check for jaundice.

Ms. Ensign was the first Ms. I ever knew. I think she was going through a divorce in a very small town, raising at least two boys, and teaching junior high girls all day long.

Yet she liberated my hair, one stitch at a time. She could have just cut the hair. It would have taken seconds. Instead, she knew that for this girl (with a bad complexion and too much height and girth to ever fit in), that hair was a source of pride. And, she knew that her job was to build up, not to tear down or cut out. She soothed me, praised the seam, admired the hair, and once I had been extricated, wrote me a pass to math.

I left knowing that I had established a new standard for what I wanted to be when I grew up. I saw a professional woman handle chaos and retain kindness, calm, and compassion. I saw a female in charge who led and nurtured at the same time, and it changed everything for me.

It was a singularity in my life. According to Professor Frank Guldbrandsen at the University of Minnesota Duluth's College of Education, a singularity simply changes everything. The dropping of the atom bomb changed everything. The invention of the wheel changed everything. That time with my hair and Ms. Ensign changed everything for me.

I had a choir director, Mr. Christianson, who had the sensitivity to make me sit up front in the bus as we returned from a contest my senior year. I hadn't received a star. I really couldn't sing very well, and I had to go home and tell my accomplished, talented, regionally-famous-for-her-voice mother that I was not a winner. Mr. Christianson let me face the road and cry quietly all the way back. He turned to me as we entered the parking lot and told me that he would call her first, before I got home. I learned in that singularity that a teacher could care about me even when I lost.

Singularities happen when you teach school. As a teacher, you will never know how many you provided. You rarely see them coming. You cannot stage them. They must be real and spontaneous, and they must come from a place so deep inside the teacher as a person that they give a student a glimpse of ethics so essential as to drive the action from the inside. They are rarely about the subject taught or the sport coached. They are not about winning or losing. They are about how you play the game, the whole game, from sunup to sunset.

Maybe the times were different then, but I remember looking to my teachers and my coaches and expecting them to live up to an unspoken code of ethics whether or not that code was enforceable. And, I don't remember that any of them did not live up to those expectations. I remember being able to count on my teachers to do the right thing, and not to flout the rules or hurt any of us in any way. As a mom, I want the same thing for my kids.

As a mom, I have implicitly asked my sons' and daughters' teachers and coaches to show my children how to be good people. Some, I have even asked explicitly. They have assured me that they would do the best they know how. It's probably not fair to expect so high a standard from folk who are as human as the rest of us, but I do. A lot of us do.

It's all in the expectations. The standard for ethical behavior is set and expected by those in charge, first by themselves and then by those whom they lead. You feel it in the expectations of the superintendent for the principals. You sense it in the standard held by the principal for the teachers. And, you know it as a student. You have seen it in your teachers.

As parents, we know it's not about the words in the contract, the talent of the performance, or the bluster and bravado and the big words. We know what matters lies in the singularities. We know that what shapes our children into honorable adults are the moments when no one is there to take names, except the children. We know that what they see enters their souls through their eyes and becomes part of who they become.

We need to count on our schools to value those singularities, to protect those souls, and to provide good lessons. As parents, we need to trust that someone up there highly values our trust and knows that our children are watching and remembering and learning all the time. Singularities add up. Children see what is rewarded, what is ignored, what is held up, and what is swept under. They see so much. And, they are always watching.

Birthday Dinners and
Long, Long Icy Fingers

●••

We are so powerful as teachers. We need to pay attention.

OVER THE PAST FEW WEEKS, I became a certain age. It's not as old as I thought it would be.

I did, however, celebrate by having dinners in restaurants—actually at least six. During two of those dinners, the conversation turned to teaching, teachers, and schools. Once on purpose, and once due to trauma.

The conversation about schools that happened on purpose occurred because most of us at that table were educators and the rest were students. The educators and students talked about what makes teachers memorable. The general consensus was that the good memories had little to do with the subject matter and a lot to do with matters of the heart and soul. The memories at that table included field trips and shopping trips, words that passed in the halls, times of reaching out, and times of protection. Specific teachers were named who had made us think, generations apart. Names of teachers were mentioned that were memorable due to bizarre incidents, or personality quirks that had become famous, for good or for ill, and had become part of the experience of the institution.

We only think we are teaching our subject area. No doubt we do, but we teach so very much more. I am so grateful that my own children have learned from their teachers that there are many ways to be adult. Teachers provide such rich diversity in the lives of our children in so many categories of learning.

The conversation about teachers that did not happen on purpose started with the turn of a head. My friend saw him across the room, and her features froze. Her beautiful eyes, in an instant, changed from their usual gentle twinkle to narrowed slits of steel. Her relaxed and happy posture became stiff. Her delicate nostrils flared, and her jaw tightened.

"I hate that man," she hissed.

He had been her teacher. Decades ago.

I don't know the particulars of why her reaction was so visceral, but I could relate. Maybe we all have had one of those, or two. Maybe I cause that reaction in some. Because I am of a certain age, I would be unlikely to see many of my nemesis teachers yet out and about, at least around here. I am so glad. I don't want to be immediately transported back to a time of powerless frustration, a time when I was wronged, hurt, humiliated, or shamed by an authority figure with a need to demean and diminish, to squash because he could.

Mine held up a drawing that I had worked and reworked (and hidden from my artistic mother and sister) of a human figure. I did not have the gifts they had. I could not see and recreate proportion in two dimensions. "Look at Julie's rubber man!" he said. He went on and on about how ridiculous and pathetic I was, in front of all my friends. I was fourteen. I had bad skin. I didn't understand the world at all, and as I write this, the tears of humiliation still rise and make their way down my cheek.

We are so powerful. Our reach, as teachers, is long and profound.

When I first began my own career as a teacher, I remember that it was OK, for some, to bang a child up against a wall, to shove a desk into a sleeping child's stomach, to intimidate by physical presence someone small and afraid. I had one of those guys who taught near me. I remember one time returning to my class and finding him in my room, with my students. He said, "I came in here, Miss, because some of these boys were getting out of line." The air in my room was thick. He was hulking over one of my boys, his big knuckles on the boy's small hands, which were pressed on the desktop. I thanked him, and then said, "I am afraid you have made a mistake. My students are all perfect. Have you ever seen anything closer to a choir of angels than these faces?" He harrumphed and left.

Those physically traumatic days are, hopefully, gone, but intimidation takes many forms. Devastation can happen with a glance, a grade used as punishment unjustly, or by way of ridicule, sarcasm, and neglect.

At a certain age, if we can still feel the icy fingers of a past cruelty, committed by someone we needed to trust and protect us, the proof of the power of what we do in our positions is nothing if not apparent. The tears, the rage, and the kindness and warmth lurk awfully near the surface.

Bull's-eyes and Secret Targets

*Being clear, up front, about what we want is a challenge for teachers.
It is unfair, however, to do less than that.*

I DIDN'T LEARN ABOUT the teaching power of a clear target when I was an undergraduate student learning to be a teacher. I didn't first learn about the beauty and simplicity of knowing where to aim as I studied to earn my master's or my doctorate degrees. No one talked about the ethics and the strengths of removing secrets as I worked to earn licenses. I can't begin to guess why.

Instead, I began to learn about clear targets by helping to raise six children. Specifically, I experienced the effects of removing vagueness regarding what I expected through years of "Room Cleaning Wars" and the advice of a long-time friend and fellow educator, Mary Lillesve, who learned it from someone else and passed it on to me. Ahhh…it took years for the smoke to clear from those agonizing Saturday morning sessions.

Our kids slept in two rooms. One held three boys. One held three girls. The deal was that no one went anywhere on Saturday until those two rooms were clean. The fighting usually began at first light.

It's not that I didn't try to be clear. I specifically would say things like, "The sheets must be changed," and "Pick up the magazines," and "No dirty clothes on the floor."

When I announced inspection, I would slowly climb the stairs as they waited in dread on their beds. I had become an enforcer, and it seemed I was always disappointed. Literature was always left somewhere. Of course, they weren't exactly magazines, so that should have been fine. The sheets on the beds were changed, yet the dirty sheets were on the floor. That was OK, according to the children, because sheets aren't clothes and I hadn't said the sheets needed to be in the laundry. There were, of course, some clean clothes on the floor…. You get the picture. I hadn't been clear.

I learned to be clearer. My friend, after working for years creating state performance standards and listening to the stories of teachers and trainers, suggested that I try a different tactic. I decided to declare the following: "Your room looks clean like a picture in a magazine (I chose the picture). There is nothing that smells anything other than fresh in there. Your room has a place for everything that makes sense. Your room will surprise and delight me, the inspector."

Defining the target worked a lot better than laying down rules or giving directions. It changed the way I parented, and it changed the way I taught. I have gradually become old and experienced enough to understand one really important thing: Moms and teachers simply cannot make a list long enough to cover all the ways that children can think. We don't all think alike.

No one can aim with confidence at what cannot be seen.

I spent this afternoon in deep discussion with a colleague trying to address those very true things. She and I worked very hard to come to agreement as to what must be in a good lesson plan. What does a plan look like when it is up to standard? Does a good lesson plan reflect a complex understanding of the student? Does a good lesson plan include alternative activities to use if the first ones bomb? Will the lesson plan pass if it only has one good activity?

Our field, like others, defines "good" in many ways. The learner too often is left to guess as to the expectations of the instructors. The learner learns to play the game, to watch for clues, to pay attention to the skills of the competition, to gauge and manipulate. Those "A's" that are allocated after all the assignments are collected, compared, and then ranked, are most often earned by those learners who have cracked the secret code and who have guessed expertly. Of course, to guess what may please a teacher, or professor, who looks like you, grew up where you grew up, speaks your language, goes to your church, and lives in your neighborhood would seem to be a lot easier than if you and your instructor did not share cultures, values, or experiences.

That's where ethics comes in. If the same people always hit the target, there should be questions and eventually some answers.

In international sports competition, such as diving, a "10" is a "10," and all of the athletes know what that means. Locally, anyone who wants to know can know precisely what is required to pass a driver's test. The scores of drivers and divers are not dependent on popularity, or on the experiences and moods of the evaluators. Their targets are visible and well defined. One can aim and hit them no matter where one grew up.

No one can aim with confidence at what cannot be seen. Students can't get there if they don't know where to go. It is unfair to define expectations after the effort is made, and it is unethical to define excellence based on criteria that has not been revealed.

This means, of course, that teachers need to know what they want. Often, it means that teachers need to agree as to what they want. Getting to that agreement is hard and meaningful work. I am so grateful to be working with colleagues willing to do that work.

I am even more grateful when I see my children with a clear target in their own studies. When the veil of secrecy is removed, so are the fear and frustration of having to guess about expectations. Then there is room for joy in learning. I can see it in their eyes. It's worth aiming for.

The Child Is the Parent of the Teacher, Too

Before we go any farther as teachers, it wouldn't hurt to consider what it is that we bring from our own school experiences to our role as educators.

AT JUST ABOUT EVERY COLLEGE CAMPUS in this country, I think, we are preparing some people to become teachers. We work hard to teach them child and adolescent development, and mastery in subject areas such as science or instrumental music. They learn educational psychology and technology, instructional methods, curriculum design, and legal as well as moral implications of teaching all children. However, I am convinced that we absolutely need to spend time working with pre-service teachers to uncover and expose the child inside the future teacher. In fact, I think that if we do not find a way to unmask and confront teachers' underlying experiences with schools, we will continue to find too many educators in classrooms who cannot see past their own pasts to recognize the vibrant importance of the lives of children in their care.

Some of the experiences of teachers as students bring huge benefits to the children in the desks, in rows, in rooms. I know that there are many students who nearly give up every year, but some adult, who grew up in similar circumstances, recognizes the symptoms, steps in, and reaches out a hand. Having a teacher promise that the breakup with the boyfriend is pain that will pass can be a lifeline. Hearing a teacher talk about living with severe acne, triumphing over painful shyness, or wearing clothes that were embarrassing reaches into the aching hearts of some students, and brings hope. Having classroom teachers that remember, who have become better because of obstacles overcome during their developing years, can and does make differences for students and provides them with examples, mentors, and heroes.

Other dark experiences of a teacher's youth, however, unless exposed, could find their way into the classroom and confuse, diminish, or traumatize students. They might even destroy the fragile, emerging adult in the children entrusted to that instructor. I remember an incident in seventh grade class. My teacher was a coach. She was leading a discussion, and I started a side conversation, again. She stomped over toward me, glaring. "Julie," she said, "You have diarrhea of the mouth!" OK. It's probably pretty tame by today's standards, but at the time it was a violent and shocking image to me, and to my friends. Up until that second, I thought words were what came out of my mouth. So did my friends and classmates. I felt inferior, dirty, and gross. I wonder what made her use that image with a vulnerable adolescent. I wonder, too, how her use of that image made me a different teacher.

We all bring our own childhood into our teaching, and our perception of teaching, for good or for ill. I would like to know how much has been resolved for those teaching my own children. What does the pompous pontificator still carry from his high school experience when he deals with my sons? What does the soft-spoken dreamer still regret as she works with my daughters? When will the power trip be over for one teacher, and when will empowerment begin for another?

When teachers see my children, do they see shadows of their own former classmates or siblings, or do they see my children? Can they rejoice in their gifts, or do they resent them? Can they empathize with frustrations and shortcomings, or will they ridicule them, or resort to sarcasm because they, themselves, were ridiculed or scorned?

One of my sons will graduate from high school this year. He wants to become a third grade teacher because his third grade teacher saw the glory, honor, and potential in him. Because of my son's childhood experience with a great teacher, he has chosen to try to bring the same sense of pride and purpose to a whole new generation of third grade children. He will carry the feeling of being seen, the soul-affirming pride of seeing himself reflected in shining promise in the eyes of his teacher. He will be defined by other, less stellar, lessons as well.

We all carry baggage. Some of it is great. Some is devastating. I'm hoping we, as teachers, find a purposeful way to recognize and build on the experiences that made us stronger and better. I am also hoping that we can find a means to exorcise the painful, degrading, and defeating experiences; learn from them; and leave them in places where they cannot harm the children we are serving now.

Bells, Bells, Bells, Bells, Bells

....

*Simple statements, like the absence of bells to mark the end of school periods,
can be profound. We are not machines, and it is good to be
reminded of that fact from time to time.*

AT FIRST, IT SEEMED like such a small thing. My son, my sixteen-year-old son, told me that there are no bells at Duluth's Central High School this year. No bells ring at the end of class. No bells ring at the beginning of class. According to my boy and his friends, not only are there no bells, but English teachers have covered up the clocks as well. The idea is that the students and the teachers need to work together until they are done.

It has always been obvious that the warming up and the waiting-for-the-bell times are not highly productive, at least as defined by educators. Therefore, this year at Central, and probably at other schools across our region, the rigor and the momentum of a well-constructed lesson can and should and will transcend the mythical, mechanical masters that bells and clocks have become.

Wow! What a simple and profound message those within the walls of such schools are sending and receiving all day long! The students are being taught not to rely on a machine, but to listen to the ghost in the machine instead. In our time of mechanical devices that can locate and summon just about any of us at any time, those students and those teachers are teaching and learning consideration and the triumph of interaction over noise.

According to Lisa Mitchell-Krocak, principal at Central, there was, at first, a fear that the loss of bells would result in an increase in tardiness and chaos—but that hasn't happened. The students seem to hurry faster to class! There are no jangling bells that signal the end of anything. There are no clanging symbols signifying the transfer of authority to the clock and the conclusion of the earned respect of pupil toward teacher. Nor are students set loose into a mass scramble until another clanging symbol establishes order.

So, the teacher, and only the teacher, is given authority to engage and to dismiss. The students, the system, and the stimulus defer to the gracious interaction that happens when human beings nurture, care, and learn from one another.

I have been so saddened, lately and increasingly, as I have watched the world of my mother slip softly away. She taught us to live in a society where folks wrote thank you notes in long hand, where we prioritized and repaid debt, and where age and wisdom were assumed inseparable and therefore always honored. I grow weary of carrying on conversations around the urgency of the cell phones' interruptions. I have become resentful of the presence of televisions in restaurants, cell phones on beaches and buses, at ballgames, and even on the Lakewalk. Must we endure the insistent, persistent, high-pitched reminder that there is something in the microwave in every kitchen, everywhere?

"Excuse me" seems to have become perfunctory and meaningless, even if it is offered by those who answer the phones and the pagers in order to pay attention to those who are not there, at the expense of those who are. The effect on me has been that I have felt insignificant compared to a contraption. I have felt that my presence and my thoughts are not what matters much at all. Day after day, year after year, the constant issuing and receiving of the message that we don't matter all that much, compared to the insistence of the devices, can only diminish our collective importance to one another.

Yet, we do have the capacity to turn off the machines and focus on the humanity. There are many cultures whose very languages utilize greeting phrases that translate roughly into "I salute your soul" and "I welcome your spirit" and "I see the great and good in you." No bell, no cell, no pager can convey any such thoughts. But, at Central High School this year, the absence of the electrical interruption is the loudest sound of all. This absence leaves space for real meaning. This year, the words "You are excused" and "Let's begin" will be heard instead. These polite and respectful phrases pull students and teachers into salutations, real reminders of what matters. At least six times a day, the "right here, right now" will take precedence. Learners and educators both will salute that which is worthy of concentration, and what is, ultimately, worth knowing and understanding.

Questioning Things We Know for Sure

What is the reason for a bell curve in the world in which we live?
We do need to stop and question those parts of our practice
that rarely see the light of discourse.

THERE ARE SOME THINGS I KNOW FOR SURE. One is that we all have some theories that provide the basis for our thinking. Those theories play themselves out in all our actions and our decisions and our triumphs and mistakes. Sometimes we can articulate those theories, and sometimes we cannot. Sometimes we are the only ones we know who hold a particular theory, and sometimes all of those we know share the same underpinnings.

Sometimes theories exist, and we never question them. We often don't question theories because we don't think about them, or we don't question them because the process of questioning would force us to change. It is, however, when we are afraid to question our own theories that theories can cripple, blind, and endanger us.

Dr. Stiggins stood up and said, "In schools, we create an artificial scarcity of success…"

Recently, I went to a conference in Minnetonka. It was the annual Minnesota Association of Supervision and Curriculum Development's Winter Conference (2005). I went because I have chosen as my life's work the field of assessment of student understanding and because the advertised speaker at the conference is one of the leaders in the field and one of my top three favorite theorists. His name is Richard Stiggins. (One of my other favorites is a gentleman whose name is Grant Wiggins, and I think it is pretty cool that their names rhyme. My other favorite is Robert Marzano, but I don't think his name rhymes with anything uncontrived.)

Anyway, Dr. Stiggins stood up and said, "In schools, we create an artificial scarcity of success, and then we make students compete for it." Well, if that isn't a kick in the underpinnings, I don't know what is!

Think about it, "An artificial scarcity of success...." For what greater good do we ever use a bell curve? Why do we decide that only some will succeed and others will not? Why do we define success in schools so narrowly? Why do the same students always end up the winners in most or all subjects? Why do we only want some to attain success so badly that we create sparseness, a scarcity of something so sweet, so empowering, so ennobling, and so encouraging as success?

As a mom, I watched our children develop gifts and interests, each unique, early on. I saw one little girl who carried books bigger than her torso into corners to read. I saw another little girl who was sidetracked at every turn by every little bug, branch, and burrowing mammal. I had a little boy who played with rope and string and tied things together to make them work with one another to create God knows what. I listened to the poetry, silly and soulful, as it flowed from the pencil of another. I watched the gifted athlete, the gifted charmer, the gifted innocent, the gifted educator, the engineer, and the consummate coach emerge from the clay that was each of them, and I stood in awe and amazement. They each had success inside them.

As a teacher, I see it, too. As the students enter my classroom, I can always see the salespeople, the ones who know how things work, the ones who are glib and witty and articulate, the ones who can create things of ultimate beauty, and those who can figure things out. I see the psychics and the psychoanalysts, the dancers and the heroes and the manipulators. I see the ones born to work with children, with animals, with the earth, and those born knowing the secrets.

Yet, I do not see all of these wonderful students succeeding in schools. I see success attributed to a very narrow band labeled "winners." The rest, whose gifts are immeasurable, struggle just to stay awake and in tune with their high school years. Their skills are not valued there.

And so, we are faced with facing a theory. Do we believe that there is a scarcity of success? Do we believe that only a few should be named the champions and the rest be labeled "those who are not"? If we believe that success should be limited, then we can remain satisfied with the bell curve.

If we believe that success can be unlimited, that all can be successful, then we need to change some pretty big systems to allow us to build on all of our children's strengths.

If schools continue to separate out the designated winners as we have done for decades, then the new question needs to be, "Who benefits from the way students are separated?" It may well be that the beneficiaries are pretty powerful. It may well be that we really do want schools to sift out some from the rest. But it doesn't hurt to ask the questions, to question the theories, to bring them out in the open. Does it?

Dancing Snowmen and Everything Else That's Wrong

We have done some damaging things as teachers without any intent to do so, repeatedly. However, once we know, once we have been asked to alter our practices because they are harmful, we can no longer pretend that we are unaware.

I HAVE BEEN WAITING FOR THIS TO HAPPEN. I remember the exact moment when I learned that it was wrong. I remember thinking that I could never go back and feel the way I felt before, or believe the way I believed before. I knew then that I would have to face it head-on one day and that I would have to take a stand, or forever bury my head in the sand with shame, and cowardice, and guilt.

And so, it came to pass that the anticipated moment happened recently. Now I have to figure out what to do about it. It's not like this is an easy, everyday moral dilemma for me. I could just make another of my normal, cowardly decisions, and carry yet another hefty bag of guilt, except that this time it would mean that I had made a Professional Chicken Decision. It's one thing to make a personal chicken decision and quite another to willingly heft a bagful of Professional Guilt. Especially when my profession is dedicated to educating children and saving the world. There's real tonnage of guilt wrapped up in this choice of flight or fight.

It started so innocently. I naively walked into an elementary school building, as part of my work, and I nearly walked into it, literally! There it was—a wall full of dancing snowmen and snowwomen. The darling little smiling snow-folk wore adorable scarves, hats, and noses made of various undeterminable vegetables. Some wore shoes that looked a lot like Michael Jordan's. Some wore earrings; others wore sunglasses. Some carried large

Balenciaga bags on their twig arms. It was obvious that each was made with a great deal of consideration and effort. Each snowperson was a work of art, created, I assume, by the child whose name was written in black crayon down the front of the three circles of snow that composed the character. Each little snow-being carried the individuality of its creator—complete with circles (that were cut either well, or less than well, by little, round, ineffective scissors) and lumps of paste with no explanation clinging to the artwork for no purpose at all.

Not that there is anything wrong with making and displaying snow-citizens named after their creators. If that was the point of the display, I could have walked away simply overwhelmed with warm, fuzzy, nostalgic feelings. What was wrong was that these were "Spelling Snowmen." These snow-individuals were dancing up a ladder of spelling success. Those who had attained the prize of perfect spelling tests were on the top rung. Those

Someone has to pull the ladder out from under our weird, entrenched need to rank our children.

who had attained lesser scores occupied lesser rungs. And, everyone knew. Everyone could see.

I remember reading about legislation that made walls and bulletin boards like this illegal. I remember reading how public display of student achievement is just plain not OK, ever, ever, ever. I have taught that law to my undergraduate students. I have discussed that law with my graduate students many times. I have assigned readings that helped them to understand the thinking behind the legislation. I have championed that thinking for many reasons.

I remember being in second grade and watching the dental cards line up on the wall above the chalkboard, and again in third grade, and again in fourth, fifth, and sixth, and the thing is, I remember that the same students were late or completely negligent in turning them in. It was always the poorest kids. I remember, even then, asking my mom why everyone in every class had to know everyone else's personal dental hygiene business.

I also remember being on the top of the list of test scores posted on classroom walls, and I remember being on the bottom. Both places brought embarrassment; one brought shame and pain as well.

Working with university students, we attempt to teach them that assessment can be used as motivation but not as punishment for children. Practicing educators soon discover that when children experience failure after failure, they no longer feel in charge of their successes or failures, and they begin to see schools as systems out to destroy them, out to get them, out to kill their spirit and take their souls. No wonder they check out in any way possible. One can only fall off the ladder so many times before one does not get up again.

I know I have to challenge the spelling snow-kids. Someone has to call an end to the hurt on the bottom rungs. Someone has to pull the ladder out from under our weird, entrenched need to rank our children. It's wrong. We need always to remember that children are made of stuff more fragile than snow and that they can drip away from us silently, sadly, and certainly, if we are not watching what we do.

Consternation and Christmas China

At my table on Christmas Eve sit two fathers, three mothers, and the children we share between us. The opportunities for misinterpretations are exponential.

THE TWENTY-YEAR-OLD COLLEGE SOPHOMORE, who had just returned home from Chicago and who just knows ever so much, looked around our table on Christmas Eve, cleared her throat, nodded at her father and her stepfather, and proclaimed, "Just think, in probably five or six years, there will be a few more alpha males at this table."

The room halted and was still. The women dabbed at their mouths and stared at her. Her brothers stifled laughs. The two patriarchs slowly put down their forks. The candles flickered. The Jell-O quivered. "Whatever do you mean?" and "Do continue!" hovered in the air.

Our bubbly co-ed cardinal chirped on about the probability of husbands and sons-in-law, and the ensuring dynamic change that would occur in our little structure. "Oh, my gosh," responded one of her older sisters, "I can easily see grandchildren in this house, but I can't really even consider husbands!"

I guess it shouldn't surprise us so much that the conceptualization of future husbands for our daughters is so much different than the conceptualization our parents conjured. This past few days, the Duluth *News Tribune* has carried stories about growing up male in our society. The stories have pointed to what educators have been watching for the past couple of decades. We are losing our boys. Lost boys, more than likely, make dubious husbands, we fear.

Don't get me wrong. I am extremely proud of my sons, and also of so many of their friends and classmates. I am privileged to teach incredibly gifted, brilliant, honorable male students at UMD. Most of the young men who have been part of our daughters' circles have been remarkable in many ways.

But then, there's the vision of Kevin Federline, the guy Britney Spears married. He may well be just a great guy, and we may have been painted an unfair portrait of his mind and morals by the tabloids, but I swear if one of our girls comes home with a dancer who dangles an eternal cigarette from his fingers with short pants barely hanging from God-knows-what near his crotch, I will lose it.

I remember a young man coming to our door, shirtless, when I was sixteen. My dad sent him home. "Not for my daughter. Not without a shirt."

I swear, I will stand at the door and say, "Not for these girls. Not without a working belt."

I see so many of them, rhetorically without working belts. There are more and more every year—boys who find schools less and less rewarding. The schools often fail to teach them in accord with how they think. Schools often categorize them as "beef" or losers. One of my sons was recently told by a teacher that, since his priorities were athletics, he shouldn't try to read difficult books because his attention span was too short. We must be so careful to nurture the scholar in the athlete, the scholar in the skateboarder or snowboarder, and the scholar hidden in bravado and façades of self-esteem.

I don't want to go back to the days when the only opportunities would go to males, God forbid. I distinctly remember being counseled to go into either nursing or teaching, myself. I am so grateful that my girls have so many more choices.

But not to pay attention to what is happening to our boys is too sad to bear. We don't need to look far to find the consequences manifested. I urge you to look at male versus female test scores for schools in Duluth, Minnesota, and Superior, Wisconsin. As the students progress through the systems, one can witness the gap widening at alarming speed. The message is clear. Our boys can't read or write like girls. Our boys can't do math like girls, either. Right here, on the shores of Lake Superior.

If we don't wake up, we could produce a generation of predominantly capable young women, and predominantly illiterate, ignorant young men, who have been taught to value transient, pointless material goods without the skills to attain them, or the reasoning to reject them.

Our faith promotes men and women as equals—two wings of the same bird. If one wing is weak, the bird flies in circles, going nowhere. When both wings are strong, we can soar.

We need alpha males and alpha females. We need matriarchs and patriarchs whose strength and wisdom have been earned by study and trial and conscious development of mind, body, and spirit. We cannot afford to neglect one gender for another. It was never the right, or smart, thing to do. We need all of our children to be strong, as partners for our daughters, and partners for our sons, and for all our generations of grandchildren to come.

Tournaments and the Real Game

....

Coaches create worlds in which the athletes learn to act. The world of a coach can be enlightening and inspiring, or harmful, to the athletes under their influence.

YOU JUST HAVE TO LOVE WATCHING THE ATHLETES, especially during tournament time. The games themselves are like moving sculptures. The teams volley across the floor, or the ice, gliding as units, with the combined value of concentration, dedication, and strength. Those that compete in postseason play at the high school, collegiate, or whatever level have entered new strata, where much is expected, and more is anticipated.

I suppose it probably is pretty unhip for a columnist to sing the praises of organized, undergraduate athletics. We writers are not particularly known for supporting such establishment clichés and often instead discuss the values of drinking in dark bars, brooding, decrying the status quo, and such. All of which is well and good, I suppose, but my work is about teaching and learning, and there is a window for just that in the lives of players and coaches that sometimes happens and sometimes does not.

I am no athlete. I did, however, grow up as the daughter of a hockey coach. My brother was a standout player, and my dad taught my sons to skate. Then he died. They took up skiing and basketball instead. My girls have done dance line and track. Whether my father told me things that could be borne out by research, I don't know, but he did tell me that his hockey players were usually full of passion, bursts of speed, and aggression, and they weren't known for being polite on intake. Basketball players were strategic, noble, graceful, and extremely athletic, from his point of view.

My dad told me that his job was to teach his boys how to channel aggression into power and speed, to capitalize on the talent of fellow players, and to differentiate between what was acceptable on the ice from what worked off the ice. By comparison, basketball coaches needed to choose a balanced team; to teach the players not to depend on the whistle off of the gym floor; and to teach them how to become part of something bigger, by giving up the ball graciously and trustingly.

The work of coaches is, from my point of view as a mother, incredibly important. In this time when many of us are raising our children without both parents at home, the coach becomes surrogate for so many missing elements in the lives of the athletes. It may not be fair, but it's real. The coach can teach plays, and that's great, but the coach can also teach children how to become adults. I have watched as my sons have learned more from some coaches off of the playing field than on, and I have watched several coaches teach lessons that I am grateful my own children have not learned.

As a mom and a fan, I have observed coaches carefully. I have cringed watching a particular coach, year after year, yell spitefully and sarcastically at his team, but what scared me most was watching his own children in the bleachers as they were unfazed by the anger and language of their father. I watched another coach send a player out deliberately to foul and harm an injured opponent, and then pat that player on the shoulder for executing an illegal and debilitating move. I have watched coaches feed into the growing egos of some players, and I have listened to a coach lie in front of players in order to cover irresponsible choices.

I have also seen wonderful acts of honor and compassion. I have watched coaches play players because they needed to see play, no matter what the score. I have witnessed coaches putting their families first, setting examples of choices that will live with my boys forever. I have listened to coaches and their players win and lose graciously, giving only credit to their opponents and kudos to their teammates.

As a teacher at a university, I see the products of great coaching in the athletes who enroll in my classes. They are almost always magnificent in their dedication both to their studies and to their sports.

There is a great difference between coaching and exploitation. As we watch athletes in tournaments, of course the sport is the thing. As the athletes go forward, into whatever their futures may bring, however, it is the other lessons learned that will remain. Those who have been coached well will reap the benefits for their lifetimes. Those who have been exploited will become resentful as they realize their glory years were not used to prepare them for better lives in a better world but for seconds of recognition by small minds and sequestered souls who believed that the moment was all that mattered.

Facing the Faces, and the Facts

....

Teaching our children to see and respond to need means
we must teach them to see their own connections to all of humanity,
and their responsibility to others.

FINDING A WAY TO CONNECT WITH OTHERS needs to be taught. I have come to believe that insulation versus participation (or resignation, resistance, and refusal versus activism, awareness, and actualization) experienced throughout childhood grows into the choices we make as adults.

As parents, and as teachers, if we do not provide opportunities and challenges to our little ones that ask of them to share, to reach out, then their choices made as adults will be limited by fear of unknowns, unfamiliarity, and ignorance of their own responsibility to respond.

It is so important for children to know and see how their unselfishness can benefit others.

It's easier, however, to just stay within our own circles, keeping our doors shut and our children arrogant.

Not too long ago, I boarded a plane returning from Mexico. A group of satiated travelers schlepped down the aisle to occupy the seats behind us, and they let the stewardess know how happy they were to be returning to Minnesota, where everyone speaks English.

"Wow," she commented patiently, but with an edge, "Did you think that because you traveled to a foreign country that the natives wouldn't speak their own language?"

Looking at who we are, and what we expect, acknowledging our sense of entitlement, and then refusing to accept a world that alienates, judges, and blames the victims takes work, bravery, and critical introspection. It starts with small, but significant, steps. It starts by setting expectations.

I have traveled with families to Mexico who brought with them their boogie boards, and their snorkels and fins, but who also carried with them a suitcase full of their children's own toys to bring to an orphanage. The blonde, freckled children from here spent time playing and reading with the children they visited. They learned to give of themselves, to give of their material possessions, and to know without a doubt that suffering and sadness exist. They also learned that there are things that they can do to make it better.

It is so important for children to know and see how their unselfishness can benefit others. It is so important for children to feel the joy of reaching past their own wants and desires to meet the needs of others. It is also important for families and schools to provide the opportunity and the protocol for experiences that bring our children face-to-face with need and with their capacity to address need.

Several years ago, as schools were trying to establish processes and procedures for combining service with learning, I remember sitting next to a former principal of a very prestigious Minneapolis prep school. Her elegance and graciousness elevated the conversation in my small group. She had been a leader, ahead of her time, because she required students to perform real, meaningful, engaged service in order to receive a diploma from her school. She politely listened as others spoke of recycling, collecting cans of food, collecting pennies, and making soap and shampoo packages tied up in washcloths. She did not denigrate the value of such projects one bit, but she did share her philosophy in designing opportunities for connecting students and need. She said, "We must have our students put a face on the masses."

I have pondered her statement over and over through the years, both as a parent and as an educator. I believe it more and more as I see the difference in students who don't see those in need as "them," but as individuals, children with whom they have played, children who hold toys that once were important to the giver, learners who have read first sentences in the presence of a young tutor, elderly individuals who were delighted to have help hanging decorations, people who held interesting and intelligent conversations over bowls of soup, and loving mothers who could keep their jobs because someone was there to watch their children.

I see the differences in future teachers who pass through my courses. There are those who cannot help but reach out and give until the giving matters, and there are also those whose first instinct is to chastise the parents, or the children, for not coming to class with advantages.

If we are ever to see change in the world, I am convinced that the change will happen one child, one teacher, and one legislator at a time. It will change when our expectations change. It will change when each suitcase of privilege is matched with one of responsibility. I believe we will become what we pray for once we are willing to look inside and model how having less means that others have more, so that we all can live abundantly as promised.

We do have to teach that our purpose here is not to receive but to give joyfully in order that we might live well. We have to help our children to see the faces of all humanity, complete with the smiles and tears that match their own.

They Are All Around Us

Where do they come from? What are they here for?

WE ARE BEING INVADED. I have seen them, sometimes in fleets, sometimes in three or four fleets a day. They arrive by the busload. Yellow buses, packed full of eager, strong, excited invaders who giggle and squirm, and eat junk food. They empty out in Canal Park, or in the castle-like playground near the aquarium, or into the aquarium, the OMNIMAX Theatre, the Marine Museum, and other points of designated interest. This city is a destination for the phenomenon of the field trip, and this is prime field trip season. I have seen buses from points west and south come into town in the morning, and leave in the evening. I love to see the little faces as they enter our city, so giddy, or so too cool, and again at about 7 p.m. as they go home, exhausted, spent, broke, and over.

A wise person once told me that it is important to celebrate beginnings and endings so that we know where we are in the passage of time. Field trips are rites of passage. There are those who see them as frills and nonsense, unnecessary spending resulting in spoiled children and rebellious youth. In times of budget cuts (which seem to be ubiquitous) and high fuel prices, etc., the field trips are often the first things to go. I hope not. Field trips are not frills; they are promises of possibilities.

I remember clearly the field trip my sixth grade class took to the state capitol. I still can see those golden horses and feel the wonderment that something so big could be made of real gold. I remember trips to the Guthrie Theater and watching professional actors tell stories, in particular an unforgettable tale of a large man named "Lenny" and a rabbit and a set of best-laid plans destroyed. I remember eating at the Nankin Café in downtown Minneapolis and pretending that I lived in that city, that I could succeed in that city, and that I wasn't afraid.

I wonder if the children visiting our city this spring are pretending, too.

It's probably human nature to get caught up in the commonplace, to place higher and higher value on what happens in the trenches and thus to lose site of the possibly extraordinary. It's easy to assume that our students are provided sufficient opportunities to expand horizons in the classroom. That assumption is insensitive.

When I was teaching Senior English Lit. and Composition in Texas, I came face-to-face with my own insensitivity and my own bourgeois assumptions, and I was justifiably shamed by a basketball coach. He was a powerful figure in our community, and he stopped by to see me after school one winter day to discuss the possible failure of two of his players. I was ready for him. I had their grades in my sacred grade book. For almost the entire quarter, their assistant coach had attended class with them, and yet those two boys showed no affinity for any of the dead, white authors I brought to them, nor had they shown any apparent attempts to improve their paragraph construction techniques. I looked this strong, popular, good old boy right in the eye and told him that he should start to really care about the levels of skills other than ball handling that these boys accrued. I asked him how he was going to feel when those boys flunked right out of Oklahoma University their first semester, no matter how well they shot or rebounded.

He listened, bowed his head, and turned to leave. Then he turned back and drawled, "Ma'am, you are not the only one who loves those boys. If they don't leave this town after this year, they will never leave. There is nothing for either one of them here. Neither one of them has ever even been to Amarillo, let alone seen how anyone else lives, or thinks. If they only last one semester, at least they will have had a chance to hear other voices and sense other expectations. I believe that if they see something better, they will believe there is something better out there, and they will do what it takes to succeed. I love those boys, too."

I humbly passed those boys. I stopped being self-righteous about field trips, and opportunities provided, and their relationships to what happened in my classroom. Classrooms house the everyday, often enjoyable, work of learning, but chances to try out new skills, new visions, and new shoes are the stuff of memories. Glimpses into worlds beyond familiar geography establish reach beyond grasp and provide for the planting of dreams. We can't cut dreams. And, we can't assume that glimpses just happen. Sometimes they only come through the windows of a yellow bus in the springtime.

Fledglings

....

Every profession has its bright and innocent, hopeful and excited newcomers.
Teaching is no exception. I fear, however, that we could do a better job
of protecting the new ones until they grow strong enough
to take on the whole task at hand.

AGAIN, THIS SPRING, I watched them fall out of the trees. Rhetorical little birds, falling out of rhetorical trees, have become predictable parts of May for me ever since I began teaching at a university. Truth is, our birds aren't really little, they are mostly young men and women, some a bit older than others, but all with fledgling experience in the profession they have chosen. They are, technically, graduates, but they are absolutely wet behind the ears; their feathers are downy, and they don't yet know what to fear, or how to challenge effectively. They have

There was a time...when plenty of people became teachers...because of June, July, and August.

not yet learned how to see through the camouflage, how to capture a shadow, or how to be wholly responsible for those placed in their care. I do, however, feel entirely confident that they will learn.

The men and women we teach in the Department of Education have chosen to become teachers. Most of these newly degreed, brand new teachers will be looking for positions. I know that in the midst of year-ending finals and portfolios, I have written my share of letters of recommendation, as have all of my colleagues. And here's the thing: I simply can't say enough good things about these people. They are so outstanding, almost each and every one of them.

There was a time, I remember, when plenty of people became teachers because they just didn't know what else to do, or because it was seen as an easy major, or because of June, July, and August. I honestly cannot say that those motivations are not present in the cohorts I have seen graduate. Yet, our students are passionate about being in classrooms, knowledgeable about the psychology of teaching and learning, and deep and current in their fields. Today's new graduates are proficient in the same technologies that permeate the worlds of their students. They are native to the milieu of the children they will teach, and they have been taught to know and respect the cultures represented in their classrooms. This year's graduates see their work as inclusive of finding a means to reach each child. They see their job as ensuring that learning happens, which is not the same as providing instruction. These new teachers have a capacity to change the world, one student and one classroom at a time, and they can't wait to begin.

So, where will they go, these downy-feathered fledglings? I have proofread letters of introduction addressed to districts in Minnesota, Wisconsin, and Texas just this spring. I have seen several letters ready to go to ISD #709 (Duluth) and to other nearby districts, as well as to Twin Cities area schools. I cannot help but wonder where they will end up. I see the incredible potential in these new teachers, but I wonder if it is apparent to others. Maybe the first work of any little bird newly pushed out of the nest is to believe in his or her own capacity and to telescope that capacity to the universe.

I suppose mother and daddy eagles can't really know for sure which of their own will absolutely survive those first months of independence. Certainly they cannot predict without inaccuracy which groundlings will eventually become the stuff of legends, the ones who will grow to be wise and elegant and symbolic of strength and skill and mastery. I have to admit that I see our new graduates and I cannot yet choose the ones who will become the teachers that get better each and every year, the ones who will teach for thirty years with intense dedication and a fire in their souls to make a difference. I don't know for sure which of their beautiful faces will smile every day, for decades, with joy and gratitude for being able to teach school well. I also don't know which new teachers will grow to become cynical, or in time, begin to blame their students, or who will be devoured by the cynicism, jealousy, or ill will of others.

I do know that there is now a batch of new ones out there who possess more skills and knowledge and understandings for sure than I had when I hit the ground. You may see them getting ready this summer. You may see some of them flying in the fall. They will be smaller and less sure than their fellow teachers, but give them time. They are made of magnificent stuff. They are the proud promise of our profession, which has always been about a great hope for tomorrow, an eye on a prize seen only through faith, and a willingness to fall and try again, and again, and again until something wonderful happens.

II. RAISING OUR CHILDREN HERE

VERYONE LIVES SOMEWHERE, either for a long time, or brief periods. Wherever we live, we are affected by the climate, the geography, the culture, and the economics of that region.

Where we live has a great bearing on the role of school and education in our lives. We live in the state of Minnesota, in the northern heartland of the USA. Minnesota has long been extremely proud of its schools and has led in innovation in public education on several fronts. In relatively recent history, Minnesota has provided and implemented ideas that have changed the face of schooling across the nation.

In the 1970s, Minnesota introduced a balancing school funding system that has been labeled the "Minnesota Miracle" because it provided a means to reconcile equity with equality in dispersing taxes to schools and students in ways that better leveled the playing field for many children.

Following the miracle, Minnesota offered "School Choice," which allowed children to enroll outside and across district boundaries. Minnesota also pioneered the creation of charter schools, public schools created to serve a specific niche or purpose.

Minnesota schoolchildren attend a combination of public, private, parochial, and charter schools, with the majority enrolled in traditional public schools. Districts in Minnesota vary tremendously in size and in resources, in geographic space, and in population concentration.

Duluth, Minnesota, where we live, is just about as pretty a city as one could imagine. It sits on the tip of Lake Superior and is the only port large enough for seagoing vessels in the state, with access (albeit a bit remote) to the world's oceans. The entire city occupies twenty-seven miles of the steep hills along the north shore of the lake, and its occupants are accustomed to strong, cold winds, wild and swift changes in weather, and the stark beauty of the blue lake, the blue sky, the white snow, and the deep green pines. The 88,000 citizens of this unique city are proud of many things, including the city's schools.

Duluth itself is surrounded on three sides by smaller cities, then smaller towns, and then the woods and the iron range to the north. If one were to drive around the tip of the lake along the southern shore, Wisconsin is right across the bridge. The city of Superior, Wisconsin, is equally proud of its schools and its flat, stretching expanses and harbors.

If one chose to drive up the north shore of the lake from Duluth, the highway is #61, of Bob Dylan's "Highway 61 Revisited." It is a famous drive with vistas so blue and wild, with splashing waves and cold spray, and crackling, booming ice and icicle formations in the cold months.

We live in a place deep in the center of the nation and the continent, yet we are connected. We are on the innermost reach of a mighty waterway's invitation to the sea and the world beyond. We live on Lake Superior, and above its blue water stretches the sky and an ever-changing panorama, rich in temptation to discover, to dream, to know, and to follow a star. We sail and ski here. We are not bound by land, yet we are rooted in traditions of mining, timber, and shipping.

Growing up here, children can simultaneously sense both the nearness and farness of the world into which they will enter. Our children's hopes and dreams are limited only by the deepest seas, the infinite height of the sky, and the boundless breadth of the vision they can conjure from where they stand.

Frost on Pumpkins and All

....

In our part of the world, one feels, breathes, and becomes the seasons.
Time passes with markers here that include a fall too brilliant and vibrant
to ever go unnoticed. Homage must be paid.

EVERY SINGLE FALL, WITHOUT FAIL, I am forced again to give Robert
Frost his due. I am still convinced that the poet was not all that some crank him
up to be. I still think that that "Two roads diverged in a yellow wood" and the
resulting "I took the road less traveled by" has become a trite justification for
self-righteousness. But, he did say, "Nothing gold can stay." And he was right.

I am, and I always will be, a recovering English teacher. I spent years
in classrooms loving teaching kids, and loving literature. I still don't feel
whole without a red pen in my purse. Part of my package is that I am often
bombarded by random brain waves that carry lines of poetry. Some are
bothersome, like "Nevermore" (Poe). Some seem silly, like "Miniver Cheevy,
child of scorn" (Robinson). Many are profound, like "'However,' replied the
universe, 'this creates in me no sense of obligation'"(Crane). Some, like
Frost's "Nothing gold can stay" are poignant. They are appropriate to the
moment, and they cause pause.

Every fall, as I see the beautiful, diverting, and demanding brilliant
colors that pop against the sapphire sky, I am acutely aware that the gold
that surrounds us can't stay. Nothing that perfect and blazing can.

My children had golden hair when they were little. I remember one fall
morning when I watched my eldest son's golden hair through a hillside of
golden birch trees. He was running to a canoe, with my husband and his friend
Roger. The three of them paddled up a river and positioned themselves so the
boy could shoot a duck. He brought down his first ever that morning. The
three paddled back through the golden haze, and he bounded, beaming, up
to the house. The boy plucked every feather and washed and soaked that bird.
The next morning, I placed it, with some wild rice, salt, pepper, and cream

of mushroom soup, in a crock-pot and hoped for the best. It cooked while we took the family to Apple Fest, and we returned to sup on that stupendous duck. It just cannot be more golden that that. It never will be that way again.

When I close my eyes, I can still see a second little boy covered completely in a leaf pile, giggling with anticipation of scaring his sisters. I can see four children on bicycles careening through yellow woods, with backpacks askew and a big white dog herding them home. I see the orange school bus emptying on our lawn, with all six of them returning home, poking each other, and racing to win nothing but the race. I smell apple pie. I watch a tired, successful garden go to rest. I smell a campfire. I hear crackling. I feel the warm earth grow colder beneath the yellow grass.

I have one more home football game to attend. I will go one more time to watch my senior boy play as the sun sets this fall. It's Homecoming, There will be the crowning and the dancing, but none of his older brothers or sisters can come home this fall. They have not stayed. Two are in India; one is in Menominee; and one is in Chicago. I cannot believe the colors are as vibrant in any of those places as they are here, right now. I cannot help but think they miss here, and us.

Apple Fest will happen. The cozy, warm, and welcoming hill that is Bayfield will welcome us once again. I will not need to herd children this year. I will not need to search for one daughter among the critters, or another among clumps of teenage boys. I will not have to ration funds for kettle corn. I will not have to decide if one can purchase hand-knit mittens, or another can climb a mast on a strange boat, or if another can zigzag his skateboard artfully amidst the crowd. I will not have to assign seats on the ride home, or stop for the girl who, according to her brother, has a bladder the size of a peanut. I will not have to collect the garbage and the stray socks from the car this weekend. Pity.

The rain pelts my windows. The golden leaves are wrenched from the trees by the determined winds. The winds will win. The gold will go.

So, we have each fall to honor and then remember. We can treasure it while it is here so close. We can etch it on our souls and then let it go.

And so, Robert Frost, again you have framed my fall. I know you will be coming back to me again soon, on a snowy evening. I can almost hear the harness bells shake.

Classrooms and Cataclysms

··

School in the fall is a routine we take for granted. Perhaps we would be
well served by considering what life would be like without that routine.

MY WISE AND STELLAR COLLEAGUE, Dr. Daniel J. Glisczinski,
successfully defended his dissertation, and that is a big, darn deal, a
magnificent accomplishment. His work, for years, has dealt with finding the
trigger to change lives, to break through students' frames of thought and force
a reconfiguration, a catharsis, a correction. Dan has looked for what causes a
learner to leave behind his or her worldview, and become forced to choose a
new direction.

His findings? It takes a cataclysm, a shaking of the whole belief system.
It takes throwing the learner off balance enough so that there is a real
possibility of falling down hard.

So, what happens after a learner is shook up? According to Glisczinski, a
learner either hides away and creates a structure of blaming, or changes beliefs in
order to incorporate a new reality. The undeniable "thing that makes no sense"
has to make sense, or the world becomes too scary, and we cannot function.

So, how do we understand an event like Hurricane Katrina, then? How
do we make sense of thousands and thousands in grief and agony, and the
heartbreaking incapacity of our resources to respond fast enough, well
enough? At first, I could not wrap my mind around her, Katrina, at all. I
could not believe it possible. I could not believe that this disaster was not
predicted so loudly that no one remained in its path.

I could not understand why there wasn't water for the poor people in the
Astrodome to drink, or contingencies for the levees, and why there were not
millions and millions of choppers in the air to lift the fear-filled, traumatized
humanity 24/7. I could not understand why Will Smith didn't fly right into that
storm and bust it up. I was so disappointed with Bruce Willis for not charging into

the mess with Angelina, Sylvester, and an army of X-Men right behind them.

Katrina is a shake-up for all of us, I hope. The fact that we didn't know—really, or didn't listen, or didn't have a plan, or enough help available, doesn't fit with what many of us understand. We need to reconfigure, reassess. We are not who we thought we were.

In Louisiana and Mississippi, millions of children will not be going back to school in the fall. Who knows when if they ever will? Our children will be going back this week. Our children will board yellow buses in the midst of golden leaves and carry their Trapper Keepers to their classrooms. Our children will gather their signatures, stand in lines, and slip into school season.

My prayer for them all this year, for all of our students, is that they will be faced in their classrooms with "things that don't fit, that don't make sense." My prayer is that every teacher brings student after student face-to-face with the inadequate assumptions and beliefs that lull us into complacency. I hope that students this school year become urgent to know more, to see more clearly, to ask "Why?" and "How do we know that?"

We should have done better for New Orleans. Maybe we can hope to teach our children not to think we are masters over everything. Maybe they can understand that we are not necessarily standing by, ready to protect and help. Perhaps they will question and examine our claim to be the most compassionate country on earth.

We can't be compassionate if we cannot see our own complacency as problematic. We can't remain delusional about our level of control and our ability to respond if we are compassionate. If we hold tight to our illusions, our current worldview, research shows that we will start to blame those victims who are already suffering more than is bearable.

Here's to the hope a new school year always brings! Here's to our kids and their teachers, and their minds, hearts, and souls, and their futures! And, here's to one thing I know for sure—they are smarter than we are, more capable of seeing through and seeing farther. I am confident they are capable of changing the world for the better, altogether. I am confident they can respond. I am confidant, Dr. Glisczinski, that our teachers and their students will not hide and blame, and become cowards on this planet. Instead, they will welcome truth over illusion, and they will reconfigure and work hard to make us ready and responsive in ways we cannot yet imagine.

Filling Them In... Sending Them Off

....

Endless forms. Endless inserting of addresses, clinics, doctors,
dentists, insurances, credit cards.
Do you suppose there can ever be just one, universal form?

WHEN IT COMES TO THE END OF THE DAY, these days, it seems my only hope is that I have filled out all the forms I need to fill out, and please, oh please, don't let too many arrive in the mail in the morning. We will have four in college this fall. Of course, no two will attend the same school. And, of course, no two will even attend schools in the same state. So, there are forms from Minnesota, from Wisconsin, from South Dakota, and from Illinois, and they all ask the same questions in different orders, using similar vague terminology, and they are all so important.

One daughter needs to write an autobiography to apply for financial aid. Another daughter needs to forward the scholarships from her high school and get vaccinated. Yet another daughter needs to check for the transcripts submitted from her semester in Australia. The son can't register for fall until we somehow clear up about twelve parking tickets he has somehow accrued in my name. He can't remember exactly why he parked where he shouldn't.

The forms are mostly on the dining room table, in four piles, next to the bill pile I can pay and across from the bill pile I can't pay. Yesterday, the soon-to-be freshman received an opportunity from her college to rent extra-long sheets for her dormitory bed. We learned a long time ago that jersey sheets from home will stretch just fine.

When the first one left for school, three summers ago, I was not just overwhelmed. I was out-whelmed by the forms, and the opportunities, and the stuff to sign. I didn't know what was expected. I didn't know what to worry about, so I worried about everything. The next year, two more of them graduated from high school, and one went to Israel and Nepal to live in service to our faith. One left as a member of a wildfire fighting crew assigned to tame the raging fires of Colorado. After that June, just going to college started to look pretty safe and tame and secure.

So, bring on the forms. I will sit and figure and fill in the blanks as best I can and send them. My life with forms for school began a long time ago, when the first one entered kindergarten. Some years, I filled out six health cards, six emergency phone cards, six picture orders. The forms changed, the addresses changed, but the exchanges remained the same.

I have and I continue to place these children I love in the hands of strangers in order that they be educated. Over time, the forms I have dutifully submitted have allowed my injured or ill children to be released to my friend Benita and brought to the clinic. Those forms have provided assistance, permission, cleared pathways, and opened the doors that have allowed my children to pursue dreams.

So, I fill them out. One after another. Over and over, I write our address, and each time, I hope someone pays attention. Each time, I want someone at that school, in that state, to understand that they can call me if they want. I will come. I will take them back if they need me. But, until they do, here is my permission to let them try to fly, far away from home where I can't see them. I will provide the information you require, dear institution, but promise you will call. You have my signature; you have this child; and once again, I will entrust my heart and hopes to whoever accepts this packet of materials. There is a mom in this envelope, you know.

Then I stamp them, and send them off, and sigh, and I so hope I am doing everything right for them all.

Watching the Boy

In loving a boy, we find ourselves humbled, confused, and honored at the site of a tree growing in our houses. The path to being a man is less clear than it was for former generations; however, some things remain the same. Rites of passage for men are part of all cultures, disguised as many things, including football.

THEY SAY THAT RARE AND PERFECT DAYS are the bailiwick of June. They, obviously, don't have a boy who plays football.

What a season! And, I know seasons. I have appeased the Football Mom gods by sitting through years of awful falls. I have frozen my naturally well-insulated butt, and blued my fingers standing on sidelines and sitting in stands, with winds blowing my coffee into my face, and sleet slicing through my blanket-tent to dribble down my nose. Oh, I am so grateful for this fall, this glorious, profligate, warm fall that has graced his senior season.

He was once the little boy who roared back at the cartoon TV monsters. When he finally started to walk, he walked off the end of the dock—harboring no fear, or sense. He was the little brother who couldn't quite keep up, but he never quit trying. He, and the dog that herded him, were always the last in the door. His older brother bonked him on the head every time he passed by, until one righteous day, when that little brother passed all of us in height. He was thirteen.

With him, it's always been about the growth thing. He was born eleven pounds, and he never slowed down. In the first grade, he was taller than his petite teacher. His gangly body flopped out of desks in every classroom, and adults always assumed he was older than his age.

He was easy to spot.

I spotted him as he practiced with the middle school team; his uniforms were always too small. I ached when they wouldn't play him. I watched him grow dejected, his whole, huge body sagging in defeat, his sadness preceding him into a room. And then I watched him become determined.

He woke up early and went to the weight room. He practiced. He trained. He dragged his sorry, aching muscles up the stairs, but he went back for more. And he continued to grow. Bigger. Stronger. Faster. He earned his starting spot, and he sweats and pounds and pushes to keep it, every day.

I make him wash his own uniforms.

For Mother's Day last spring, he made me a card. It said, "Mom, I'll always have your back."

He plays for Central High School, and last Saturday, the Trojans won a really big game. The sun shone on those boys on the field, and the stands basked in the warmth. The air was crisp, like a cold apple. I sat amidst the same dear-hearted moms and dads, aunts, uncles, and grammas that I have sat amongst for six years. Rocky's dad once carried my bleeding boy away from a game to the hospital, and he and Rocky's mom kept him overnight when I had to be away for work. Alex's uncle sent him a card that claimed he spotted potential when my boy was a sophomore and full of self-doubt.

Chuck's mom feeds my boy more than I do. When these boys hang out at our homes, they mostly eat. It's not light duty to feed any one of them. En masse, feeding requires tonnage. The bountiful reward of having those boys in the house, however, is immeasurable.

The stands were full of color. The students wore face paint, helmets, boas, and combinations of red, white, and black in infinite intertwinings, bursting with fancy, and pride, and creativity. There was the blasting, ebullient band, the gleeful cheerleaders, and pretty much, all was right with the world.

We won. Our boys will go on to play for the Section Championship on Friday. We watched them leave the field, exuberant, climb on the bus, triumphant, chanting and waving pads and jerseys out the windows.

After they were gone, and I finally remembered where I parked, I drove home. I was not paying attention, so I missed my exit and had to backtrack about twenty blocks through quiet streets. I went in to the silent, dark, cool house, and puttered and putzed for about an hour, listening to the tick of the clock, and the rustle of the leaves, and nothing else.

The phone chimed. I picked it up to hear his big voice, deep and echoing, as if from the belly of a whale. "Mommie," it said, and it reverberated off the cupboard doors, "Did you see us? Did you watch me play?"

Action, Justice, Jefferson,
and Clayton, Jackson, McGhie

*In Duluth, a group of citizens armed only with incredible dedication and
a cause that spoke volumes to many, managed to secure funds to build a
remarkable sculpture on a lot in the middle of the city that reminds us all of the
lynching of three innocent African-Americans accused of rape, not so long ago.*

YOU CAN JUST GO CHECK IT OUT FOR YOURSELF if you like. Today,
my horoscope actually said, "Sitting at home thinking about what you would
like to do to change the world won't make it happen." I am a Cancer, and I
have come to understand, after being a Cancer for fifty-plus years, that we
are the least glamorous sign in the entire Zodiac. While other signs warn of
unfaithful lovers and predict wild romance on the beach for hours and hours
without getting tired, my daily messages from the stars are inevitably related
to finding something nice for the home or staying at home for another in an
endless series of quiet and peaceful evenings, surrounded by the nice things
I supposedly have found. But, today's message told me basically that staying
home, as I have been so often directed, would not change the world. So, I
went out.

In truth, I would have attended the Clayton, Jackson, McGhie Memorial
Remembrance Event no matter what my horoscope said, for myriad reasons.
I am amazed and awestruck by the power of the monument in downtown
Duluth. I am equally amazed and awestruck by the power of vision that the
small group of volunteers who conceived of the idea of commemoration
had, to make such a remarkable dream a reality. I have had the honor of
assisting this committee, and they are magnificent in their dedication and
in their passion for social justice. I am so proud of us, as a city, for setting
aside a beautiful, strong, consecrated spot for reflection and remembrance

and realization, right on First Street. I also went because two of our children danced in the program.

When I got there, I followed the small crowd into the Encounter Building, up to the old Shrine Auditorium, because it really looked like rain. I turned around and saw so many familiar faces of Duluthians who may not know exactly what is the best, most effective path to take to end social injustice and racism, because nobody does, but who keep trying despite the obstacles. The Mayor spoke of the wrongness and racism of homelessness in our population. A talented young man sang Dylan's "Desolation Row," and Catherine Ostos spoke about forgiveness. Catherine said that it doesn't mean you need to condone to forgive, and that it is forgiveness that heals. She told us that even if right is on our side, we should apologize for our self-righteousness and open the means

The lynching happened here. And the monument happened here.

to communicate and understand. I think a French proverb reflects her message. It says, "To understand is to forgive."

But, forgive and forget are not the same thing. Maya Angelou said, "History, despite its wrenching pain, cannot be unlived, and if faced with courage, need not be lived again."

We are surrounded by history in this city. But the immediacy of the Clayton, Jackson, McGhie Memorial, right downtown, gives this piece of really dark history in our city power to help us not to live it again. We are reminded by this site that it was the town folk, the people who may have lived in the houses we now occupy, who may well have downtown buildings named after them, who did the lynching. It was church people, teachers, lawyers, moms, dads, grandparents, sailors, and factory workers and everyone else who dragged those innocent men into the street and hung them until they died.

This week we were told that the city moved the statue of the oldest Civil War veteran from Canal Park to somewhere else, and I couldn't help but wonder if he was at the lynching, too. Do you think the presiding mayor and mayors of this city that followed, the ones who so insightfully saved the green spaces from development, who provided us with parks and trails and incredible civic beauty, were there, too? Do you think the owners of the mansions we admire were there? We have seen pictures of the crowds, and there were many, many people, and we know they were not all from out of town. I live in a little house that is over a hundred years old; did those who built my house attend the lynching? Did they bring their children?

One of the beauties of our monument is that it raises the question of "Who did this?" and the answer is unequivocally, "Us." The monument says, "We will speak of this." It asks forgiveness, but not forgetfulness, and it does not hide behind the cloak of mythical heroes and impossible men. It reminds us that history is made of events and decisions made by real people in real situations, and that there are no superheroes destined to swoop in at the last minute and make right happen. It reminds us that we are all vulnerable to the dark side of our natures. By seeing history as a struggle between those natures, we give our children the power to overcome intolerance and injustice simply by admitting that unless we stop it, it will not be stopped.

The lynching happened here. And the monument happened here. The admittance and reminder of the duality of our use and abuse of power exist in this place downtown. It is humbling, and it is this humility that could make studies of history so much richer for our schoolchildren. According to the book by James W. Loewen, *Lies My Teacher Told Me* (1996), Patrick Henry, the man who so famously proclaimed, "Give me liberty or give me death," owned slaves. Thomas Jefferson, the man who asserted that everyone has the right to "life, liberty, and the pursuit of happiness," actually owned and enslaved 175 human beings at the time he wrote those words! We are a nation, a world, of many crippling dualities, duplicit rhetoric, and dubious, all-too-human heroes.

If exposed to the reality that the causes and the perpetuation of social injustice come from within our society, within our very cities, possibly from our neighbors and friends and community leaders, our children could actually become empowered to do more than sit at home thinking about what they would like to do to change the world. They could lead the way to making it happen.

A Theory of Crabbiness

After fall, the cold begins. Some see it as wicked and threatening, others rejoice in its extremeness. It is what it is, and what it has become to all of us.

I HAVE A THEORY as to why we are so crabby around here when there is not a lot of snow on the ground in January. I am not discounting the fact that no snow is just dirty and gross. I am also aware that a January this warm can't not be indicative of global warming. I know, too, that sticky, wet snow and patches of bald dirt do not make for great skiing. All that, of course, but I also think that no snow is robbing us of our cocoons, and that is a dirty shame, indeed!

I mean rhetorical cocoons, not biological ones. We all know that the cocoons of moths and butterflies are miracles of transformation. In goes a worm; out comes a wonder. Those creatures create for themselves a shelter in which to become something else. No one expects the caterpillars to exchange cellular structures and continue to grow gardens, buy groceries, clean houses, or drive kids around. No one expects the caterpillars to make tough decisions, balance checkbooks, or even shovel as they sprout wings and legs.

I think a heavy blanket of snow allows us here in the North to burrow in and work on ourselves for a while. I think that a soft and white cover forces us inside, both physically and psychologically. Just as we know that under the surface of the snow there are creatures scurrying about, eating my daffodil bulbs, we also know the potential of what can happen inside as we sit and watch out the windows. We may look inactive in deep snow, but it is the true winter that allows transformation. Each snow season, we have the possibility of emerging anew in the spring. Under the surface, without everyone watching, we can become different.

I don't know how folks in warm climates do it. I imagine there are those who can go outside, pick a mango, and then surf and self-reflect. But, my theory is that we have been conditioned, even in a culture such as ours where we don't talk about self-growth much, to use the winter, the soft still darkness, to think.

I am watching my students come back to the university to start a new semester. They will sequester themselves away from home in this cold season and hunker down over their books and computers and emerge with new understandings in the spring. The students in the high schools and middle schools and elementary schools will do the same. This time, between now and sometime in April, is the most concentrated time of learning for students at any level.

We are all, most likely, students this time of year. Our geography rather forces us into the mode of absorbing during these months. Perhaps, because of this hibernation, we are really lucky. We are usually provided with a snow cocoon, and we get stressed out when nature is not delivering on promises made on precedent.

According to William Bridges, in his classic work *Transitions: Making Sense of Life's Changes* (1980), adults continue to grow and become wise through transformation after transformation. Transformations, however, are often painful, and always difficult. They consist of three distinct phases that begin with an ending. We all need first to accept that something has to change. We have to say farewell to who we have been. The second phase of adult transformation Bridges calls "The Neutral Zone," and it is a cocoon. This is the time of self-reflection, acknowledging inadequacies, and taking responsibility to learn different ways of being. The third phase is that of new beginnings, taking risks with new skills.

I am sure we all can name people, or cite our own experiences, to give examples of opportunities for transformation that didn't result in growth. I know I have watched winters, divorces, deaths, career interruptions, births, and graduations that have resulted in no new understandings, outlooks, or insight. And I have witnessed cataclysmic events that produced wiser, more incredible individuals. The difference in the experiences was not the experience itself but what the person did with the experience. Crucial to the gaining of growth is the neutral zone, the cocoon, the time when we gently own our need to change and take real action to make that change occur. Skipping the cocoon results in blaming others. Going inside and thinking in the dark and pain, dealing with the anger, and reflecting in the stillness produces the butterfly.

I don't want this whiteless winter to go by without that time of reflection. I believe many of us have come to depend on the cold nights to shed some light. Perhaps we will need to pretend, close our eyes, and imagine the sweep of a snowy wind against the empty swing set. Creak. Swoosh. Shhh…

Walking Uphill in the Dark

....

In the midst of winter, one early morning in 2007, students from Duluth's Central High School took it upon themselves to walk through the city from the lakeside, tracing the route that many of their classmates were forced to walk every day in the cold, ice, and rain. The walkers were concerned that their classmates were missing too much school due to the difficulty of the daily climb up the hill. They were accompanied by teachers, parents, and some representatives of the local media. As a result of the demonstration, bus passes were provided to the Central Hillside students at no cost.

INTEGRITY IS SUCH A TOUGH CONCEPT TO TEACH. I imagine every person on earth has an individual definition of the word (which makes teaching it pretty problematic to begin with). Yet, I cannot imagine that we wouldn't want to raise young people who can recognize it, and value it.

I know integrity when I see it, sometimes. I think I know when I don't see it.

I saw it last Thursday, as thirty or forty Central High School students, teachers, and parents walked the walk, up the hill, from down by the lake, to school. It was cold, but not as cold as it gets many mornings. It was crisp, but it wasn't sleeting, raining, or blowing like stink. They left early in the morning and arrived at school on time. They walked the path required of many Central students living in Central Hillside every day, day in and day out, to get to school.

The students who walked last Thursday were mostly not from the neighborhood. They were from all over, and they were walking to make people aware of a problem. They walked to bring a bad situation to light. They walked because they believed that the presence of all their classmates in school matters. It's not OK that some students have to walk nearly two miles uphill, in the dark coming and going. It's not OK that some students cannot participate in music or sports because it's just too hard to tote an instrument and equipment day after day. It should not be OK that those who can afford bus passes have an unfair advantage.

They walked, with backpacks, from the Rose Garden to school. Students who live on the way up the hill make that walk daily, in the rain, dark, cold, and snow. The walkers crossed Mesaba with an escort. Steep Mesaba Avenue can be a slippery disaster some days. (I have a friend who lives toward the bottom, and she and her husband sit at the window on icy days. She says it's like watching bowling, the way the cars slide and collide with one another.)

The walkers were warmly dressed, which is not always possible for all students, and they were in no big rush, which is also not always the case for the daily walkers.

Amongst those who made the walk was a personality from a local morning radio show. He was invited by one of the parents on Central's Site Council, and he certainly deserves credit for making the effort. His position was that the uphill, dark walk is good for the students. I suppose it's the old "When I was in school we walked thirteen miles in

> *The Central students were not walking to draw attention to themselves, but to an issue.*

snow uphill both ways" deal. He did have to admit, however, that he had super warm clothes on that would have been tough to store if he had been a real student. He also carried a real student's backpack briefly and was astonished at the bulk and weight of the thing.

The radio guy asked questions of the walkers, and they answered, knowledgeably, about absences among students who make that walk daily, about the price of bus passes, about why they were out there. The Central students were not walking to draw attention to themselves, but to an issue. They were there to try to make a difference.

That, I think, is integrity.

Integrity is not about drawing attention to a personal issue. It is also not about using attention for its own sake. Integrity, I believe, is about researching, understanding both sides of a story, and then doing something about it.

There are folks who use attention, and access to press, to pass off personal opinions as if they were truths. There are individuals who rant with only half the story, or worse, who ignore half the story, or choose to report half the story while claiming to break news. There are those whose understanding is so limited that they become pathetic.

This kind of reporting happens in all fields, but it seems to be particularly prevalent in reports about school issues. It is too often the case that attention seekers who have attended school think they understand the large and complex systems that they are. Because school officials protect people and integrity, those with little knowledge can misconstrue that protection.

Another way to draw attention is to scream "Danger" or "Misappropriation" or "Failure" in headlines. But, unless those screamers are willing to walk a mile, or two miles, uphill in the dark, in the shoes of those who take the time to really understand, there is no integrity in their diatribes.

The heroes are the kids and faculty and administration of Central High School, and everyone else who walked last Thursday morning. My heroes also include the solid integrity of District #709 leadership, whose grace and dignity protects the rights of those students to march and be heard, above the din, for all the right reasons.

Too Cold

If we grew up in the Northland, we know about the anticipation of the announcement. We know why we watch the crawl on the screen, and the reaction to the news depends, of course, on the level of preparation and contingency we understand.

THERE WAS NO SCHOOL TODAY. It was just too darn cold. It was just too darn cold for anything.

I watched my university students file in this morning at 8 a.m. or so, and they were moving pretty slowly. Like molasses, as my dad used to say.

They were bundled up, my wonderful elementary education majors, wrapped in fluffy mittens, giant coats, warm sweatpants, and one even showed off the cuffs of his long johns. Their hands were wrapped around mugs of insulated hot chocolate and coffee as they huddled in their seats, waiting, knees to their chins, cozy and safe, munching on the donut holes and blueberry bread that I brought for them.

"So," they asked, "Why do we have school if the K-12 schools are closed? Why is it too cold for them, but not for us?" They may even have thought I had the one right answer.

Of course I did not. I can guess. I believe that our superintendent did not have school today because it was just too darn cold. I don't think it was because the buses would not start, or because the buildings would be too expensive to heat. I don't think it was an economic decision at all. My thinking is that the decision had to do with little children waiting outside for rides to school. It was just too darn cold.

I am sure that most of us remember the utter joy and delight we experienced due to an announcement of an unexpected day of freedom, of vacation due to weather. For many of us, it meant a day to ski, or skate, or hang out, or lie around the house and talk on the phone. The forecast of a blizzard was always accompanied with a fist full of hope...maybe no school! Hooray! We might be able to play on the mounds of snow that touched our rooftops. It might mean that we could make cookies, or popcorn, or home-baked beans. The possibilities were endless and full of happy choices.

Some of the same possibilities probably faced my students this morning. If the university had called off school, they could have stayed in their rooms, made hot chocolate, or they could have dressed well and carefully and gone snowboarding.

I used to see these cold days as offering only happy options. And then, of course, I grew up a little.

One day, about six years ago, we had a snowstorm on a school day that fell just a tad short of being worthy of a surprise holiday. I was scheduled to be at one of our elementary schools for a meeting, so I drove in from the country, with little visibility, sloshed and fought my way through the strong, laden-with-snow, biting wind, and entered the building along with the children in the morning.

As my eyes adjusted to the dim light in the hallway, I saw the children clearly. There were boys with runny noses in floppy hats and macho mittens, and girls in puffy coats and macho mittens, too. But there were also girls in dresses with no tights, just bare legs in tennis shoes. There were boys with no mittens, no hats, no scarves, no boots. There were children dripping as they thawed, who were wearing summer jackets, and some had no jackets at all. They were so cold.

It was not their fault. Nor was it the fault of the parents, who most likely had to leave for work long before their children left the home. It was also not the fault of the parents or the children if it was just not possible to get a coat this month. It is not a matter of fault. It is, however, a matter of fact.

On days school is cancelled now, I cannot help but wonder and pray for those children. Where do they go on snow days? How do they stay warm in this bitter cold? What can we do to make it better for them and their parents? What can we as a city, state, and nation that claims to value children more than any other resources actually do to keep them warm, and cozy, and safe?

My students will grow up, too. They will see the red fingers, the blue legs, the lashes, and chapped lips. My hope, of course, is that someday, before too long, we can feel a whole lot better about how we keep our promises. Wouldn't it be easier to handle this cold if we knew that no child would be left behind, outside, without warm clothes? Wouldn't it be just a giant step in the right direction if we knew that mothers at work would not be terrified for their freezing children on their way to school?

Wouldn't it be great to rest assured that our warmth and capacity to be cozy was the reality for every child? Even when it's too darn cold? Especially when it is too darn cold?

Red Lake

··

Violence in schools is a violation of so much that we hold sacred.
There was Columbine, and other tragic scenarios both before and since.
In Minnesota, there was Rocori, and then Red Lake.

WHAT CAN WE SAY FOR RED LAKE? What can we say, or think, or do, or feel for such an indescribable event? Words fail.

I do know that every single time that I have asked any parent if they ever thought they could love anything as much as they found themselves loving their children, the answer has been, "No, I never knew how much I could love until they came into my life." Once you know that love, that joy, that promise, there can be nothing that could ever replace it. That loss can never be grieved enough, not ever.

It is, perhaps, our common understanding of universal motherhood, or parenthood, that makes me want to go outside in the moonlight and wail and caterwaul into the west in hopes that some wind will carry my feelings to Red Lake, to join the tears that are there.

It is that same understanding that wants to shake the shoulders of those who sit in cafés and behind news desks and assign reason to such madness. Can't they see? This unspeakable tragedy is not because of anything. It does not have a motive that could mitigate. It is not because of gun control (the killer used police weapons), nor is it because of lack of security or lack of morals or anything easily blamed. It just happened because there is insanity in all of us and in unjust measure in some of us, and perhaps that insanity is growing in our midst and is fueled by many factors.

There is no simple answer in Red Lake, or Rocori, or Columbine, or anywhere that children and teachers are murdered in schools. There is no easy solution. We are all bound in these events with a sense of hopelessness, and vulnerability, and common humility.

The morning's newspaper had a picture of three beautiful girls from Red Lake, holding one another. Their faces were seeking, and streaked with tears. When each of them had left for school that morning, their families could not have known that this is how the day would end. Those girls were not sent to school to see blood run in the halls.

The news story told of the tragedy. One of the teachers interviewed was my own student not too long ago. She was a wonderful student who loved her work and adored her students. It seems she barricaded students in her room, according to the news. I can't help but imagine her, her kind face and her voice of experience, bravely creating a barricade to protect her students as best she could, filled with terror, waiting, waiting.

As teachers we know that when parents send your children to us that you expect us to protect them. We know that you expect us to protect them from bullies, and bad words and bad thoughts and bad self-esteem, and we do our best. But we don't know how to protect them against this. We do know how you love them. We love them. But we don't know how to promise their safety in the face of such random rage. We will build barricades, and we will take precautions, but the rest is unbearable. We cannot bear the unbearable, either.

And so, what can we say to Red Lake? We cannot speak. We can only humbly turn and reach out our hands and call "Brother!" and "Sister!" We can pray that the brothers and sisters and mothers and fathers and grandparents and all who love those lost are somehow provided courage in measures I know I could never attain, just to go on and be there for one another. And we can pray that Red Lake transcends human understanding to find some solace for these indescribable, inconsolable murders of such hope, and such promise, such innocence and such beloved individuals.

I cannot know what else to say. I am so sorry.

Brave Hearts and the Boardwalk

....

There is nothing like spring north of Central Minnesota. We are so grateful.
We are a place on a Great Lake, and spring brings us back in touch with the
passageway to the oceans that made this city vital for trade,
and continues to keep this city alive and connected to the world.

OMIGOSH, I WALKED THE LAKEWALK ON FRIDAY! What a glorious thing! I am not a Lakewalk Diehard. I try to walk it regularly during warm weather, but come fall, I die easy. I need to have the Lakewalk work with me, and it was working on Friday evening. It was warm, it being just spring, and I and my friend and about four thousand others were out there, next to the lake we love, spotting for little green sprouts and imagining a faint green haze just above the treetops.

If you were out there, you probably saw us. I walked with a colleague, and we were so psyched. We walked fast, and we are both tall, and we talk with our hands, both of us, with our hands out in front of us, drawing on imaginary boards and providing invisible brackets in the air just about every-

Of course, the idea of the heart and the mind being intertwined is certainly not new.

where. If you grew afraid as we approached, I apologize. But we were just so happy to be outside, and warm, and she is so into a new train of thought in our profession that we probably were intoxicated with just the pure joy of it all.

Spring does that. After a winter in classrooms, leaving home in the dark and returning home in the dark, the idea of life renewing and light increasing makes for all kinds of giddiness. As I drove into campus today,

I saw a young man basking in the sun and blowing his trumpet in the front yard of the Weber Music Hall. This is the time of anticipation of little blossoms everywhere. This is the time when hearts leap.

My colleague talked to me on the Lakewalk about hearts. She has been reading about the connection between the heart, the actual and the mythical organ, and learning. She works with teachers who work with children who have barriers we are only beginning to understand, whose difficulties land somewhere on the spectrum that has been identified as Autism Spectrum Disorders. She is excited about another window. She is excited about another way to maybe reach these children. It's spring in her world as hope is renewed again. There may be another way to plant the seeds, another chance to see new growth.

Of course, the idea of the heart and the mind being intertwined is certainly not new. What we know now about physiology and neurology may simply prove what we have always known on a deeper level. I think we have always known that learning is a natural act, that knowledge is of value to the heart and the mind and the spirit, and that wisdom is earned by processing information through the heart and the soul, through trial and error, through failure and triumph. What we know comes to us first through the senses, and who we are decides how that sensory information will be stored and interpreted. What we understand is, and always has been, a function of more than simple neural connections.

Several years ago, I traveled to Greece and toured the Parthenon. It is a hill topped by temples, in the heart of the city of Athens, built by the ancient Greeks to honor Athena, the Goddess of Wisdom. It stands still, incredibly beautiful, carved of white marble, proud and exquisite. Our guide led us up the many stairs, carrying a heavy backpack. When she arrived at the top, she sat on a rock facing the temple of Athena Nike. She opened her backpack and took from it a huge bag of cat food. At least twenty feral cats leapt to her seat, rubbed up against her legs, and purred and perched on her shoulder. She petted them and stroked them and turned to us and explained that we can't expect anything, cat or child, to honor the Goddess of Wisdom unless they are first fed and loved. Feed the body. Feed the heart. Feed the mind.

This is certainly not new thinking. All cultures have looked and continue to look at how the world works from where they stand and to interpret its workings through their own lenses. All sciences watch nature, observe its intricacies, and interpolate their findings with what is already known and understood. I believe that all cultures build monuments, establish worship, create art, or somehow show respect for that which we yet don't know but may know someday. The Greeks built temples and established places to learn. The Egyptians created libraries. Many peoples carefully passed down oral histories in order that sacred and secular understandings were preserved. From the Lakewalk, one can see old, beautiful, venerated Central High School. It is a magnificent reminder, right in the heart of our city, of the value we place on learning and the promise that future generations will understand more than we do now.

And then comes spring. We watch things grow where there was no sign of life. We are reminded that the heart of the earth kept life safe through the bitter cold, and we know that nothing is too hard. We only need to find the right combination—the right seed, the right soil, the right light, the right timing, and things can be green and flourish, everywhere, absolutely everywhere!

Maybe my friend's new insights into her work will bring forth wonderful results. Maybe some children will be better served. Maybe nothing will come of it. But the fact that we get giddy over the possibilities reminds me what a strong thing with feathers this hope is, this idea that all children can and will learn well. It flies before us, and it can see farther than what we know. It's like just spring, full of possibilities and packed with promise. New insight still brings to those who work and wait and watch such full to bursting hearts that they float along the Lakewalk and flutter through the rooms of the clinics and the schools, and down the halls of the universities, like butterflies and fresh air and welcome sunshine.

Robins and Coffee Spoons

···

What marks our lives as parents? The details get in the way.

T. S ELIOT'S HERO OF SORTS, J. Alfred Prufrock, claims to have measured his life in coffee spoons. Sometimes, I feel the same way. I sure do think I have spent an inordinate amount of my life in meetings, stirring the powdered, dehydrated cream into my coffee. I am not even complaining, as I would rather have spent that time stirring than, perhaps, attempting to change truck tires in the mud or any other work activities that I do not know how to do. I can also imagine that there are many, many people who would much rather do just about anything than sit in a meeting. Nonetheless, meetings are what shapes policy, drives change, and provides communication channels for much of what happens in bureaucracies, and education is a bureaucracy without a doubt.

I sat in a meeting this morning and listened and spoke and opined and listened so that I understood, and right in the middle of my own sentence, I saw a robin outside in the courtyard. It was a pretty scrawny robin, I have to say, and its breast wasn't sensationally orange, but it was there, on the branch, and I at once realized that I was another year older, and so are my children. This realization did not stop me from making my most likely very important point, but it did hit me later, as I chomped down a wrap of some sort for lunch in front of my computer screen, reconfiguring a matrix in preparation for another meeting. Somehow, in the midst of crises, and coursework and classes and current events, another year has slipped by. I have nearly completed another year of school, for my self and with my children. So, what happened?

I started this fall by picking up football gear, pads and funny socks, off of the floor by the door, and somehow the uniform changed to giant basketball shorts, and now I am finding smelly track clothes in gym bags. I started by watching clothes and suitcases leave for colleges, and now I can see that they will return. I observed the registrations, wrote the checks, sent in the notes for absences, checked over the report cards, and last weekend, I attended the Central Pop Concert. I watched the beautiful girls and beautiful boys in their formal attire as they sang their hearts out and played their hearts out and were so remarkable in their performances. I wonder if their directors measure their own lives in rides on the moveable stage and in loading vans full of instruments.

The sad part is that I don't think I savored it enough this year. You would think that, with four of them gone, I would have accrued enough experience to have learned that these years are so precious, that the concerts and the conferences and the conversations are privileges, and priceless, and they don't last. But I don't think I have learned this lesson well enough. I let that darn robin take me by surprise. I have let this year go by in coffee spoons and appointments, and I can't get it back. I have not been as wise as I should have been.

If I had known then what I know now, if I could have lived this year over again, I think I would not have spent so much time in meetings. I think I would have spent more time with my children, just sitting beside them, listening. I wish I had written more things down that they said this year, that they did this year. I wish I would have recorded, chronicled their hopes and dreams for the year and then their triumphs. I wish I would have looked at them more and studied their faces. I wish I had been more observant and more astute.

If I could take back several years, I know I would take more pictures, keep more of the refrigerator art and the writing assignments. I would have taken better notes, kept stronger journals and written poetry, inadequate poetry, about my children. I know I would remember more now if I had done a better job then.

So, the robin has come, and this year in schools is wrapping up. I am grateful for the wake-up call the bird provided. Perhaps at least I can gather and nest a bit. Perhaps I can find the pictures at the bottom of the backpacks, salvage the papers from the piles, and print out a few of the writings that sit on the desktop and save some things to represent this year. I know that these days, when school years are the measurements, will end. I know that I will have years, soon, when I no longer have children in the Pop Concert. I will have years when I will no longer pick up gear of any sort off the floor by the door, and I know that then the meetings and the coffee spoons will be pretty empty reflections of the abundance evident in the promise of spring and parenting schoolchildren.

Latin, Lessons, and Lift

Commencements happen every spring in high schools everywhere.
However, when one of your own is in a cap and gown,
it is difficult to remain at all apart, unafraid, and only hopeful for the future.

TONIGHT WE WATCHED NUMBER FOUR FLY AWAY. We have watched three before her walk across the stage, shake hands, shake hands, shake hands, receive the scroll that says, "You have completed Central High School" (or something like that), descend the steps, and change everything. Tonight, our beautiful, little blonde bird bounced, smiled brightly, twirled, perched for a second at the edge of the stage, and then took flight. She is no longer a high school student. She, along with all of the graduates from all of the high schools this spring, has begun the task of defining a generation.

I sat in the audience at the Duluth Entertainment and Convention Center and looked at the faces of the superintendent, the school board members, the principals, the advisors, and the counselors, and I wondered if they felt secure. I wondered if they felt sure that what they have provided will suffice.

> *She, along with all of the graduates from all of the high schools this spring, has begun the task of defining a generation.*

How did they know, thirteen years ago when she skipped through the doors of Nettleton Elementary, what she was going to need to know tonight? How could anyone have seen the world we see from back then?

Our girl will be part of what has been called the "Millennial Generation." It is said of this class that they will insist on solutions to the accumulated problems and injustices that they have inherited from us. It is said that this group embraces technology, feels its power and holds firm the reins, and sees its potential to usher in a new age. This group will be part of a nation of minorities, where social and intellectual capital will be highly prized and actively sought and recruited. It is also said that this generation will not settle for quick fixes, nor will they defend the status quo. Instead, this generation will work for continuous, steady improvement in a climate of intense competition and breakthrough thinking.

If so, how did they learn to do all that? Where did they learn to harness technology and ride its strengths? Who taught them to listen and value and learn from the best of all cultures and experiences in order to recognize breakthrough thought? When did they pick up the skill to avoid quick fixes and to implement systematic solutions? How on earth did they gain the insight to value intellectual capital?

There was a time, between my school years and my little sister's, when my high school stopped requiring a year of Latin. There was a time when keyboarding became required. There was a time when it was determined by someone that all of us no longer needed to be able to explain the Smoot-Hawley Tariff, but we did need to be able to define a binary system.

I still maintain that we should have kept the Latin. I sincerely believe that I am a better person than is my sister precisely because I can conjugate a verb in at least five dead languages. Be that as it may, none of my own children have studied Latin. They did learn how to write, however, from those schooled in the classics. Four of mine learned to love and see and romance words under the guidance of Cal Benson, a well-loved faculty member and an institution at Central. This year he retired, and someone else will teach our remaining two. Will they learn what their siblings know? Will they know enough? Do we know enough to perpetuate what matters and de-emphasize the trivial in order to make room to teach and learn what will be required to survive and thrive in a world we will not live to see?

More important, can we do it quickly enough for the next group of graduates? I watch school boards and administrations debate, decide, and then step back from decisions, and I worry that we are wasting time. Wave after wave, class after class enters and leaves, and each group will face a world where the speed of things increases exponentially. We need to see that speed and rejoice in its exhilaration and match it in our readiness to prepare our children for its implications.

Revisiting, revisioning, and envisioning need to happen continuously and systematically in our schools. This Millennial Generation will soon be sending their children to our schools, and we will need to create processes and procedures that ensure the valuing of intellectual and social capital and that lead to solutions to the problems we have debated but not solved. Our schools and our expectations have produced graduates that will hold us to higher and swifter and more competitive standards. We will meet them, or they will find other answers. We will have to work harder and skate faster if we intend to be where we need to be. So, we will. Much depends on our ability to predict and react, to value and invent. So, we have to.

I did notice tonight that not one of the graduates looked behind as they crossed the stage. To a person, each one looked ahead, faced forward, smiled, and gathered speed as they went off to become what they will become. They are magnificent in their courage and in their strength and in their faith in the future. What power they hold in their exuberance! How blessed we have been to be part of their passage and to continue to serve those to follow.

Knowing Enough

....

*Letting go and being OK with that are simply words spoken by someone who
probably never had to do so. During spring of any child's senior year,
letting go and paralyzing fear go hand in hand.*

I WONDER WHEN I will be smart enough to be the mom I wish I were?

When I was mom to my first, and second, and third seniors in high
school, I honestly believed that I would have it figured out by the time the
fourth and fifth ones came around. But I didn't, and I don't. I do think,
however, that spring of the senior year is probably as tense as it gets, overall,
in the scheme of things, as far as parenting goes.

Of course, I don't claim that spring of senior year compares to the trauma
and impossibility and the heart-wrenchingness of being a parent during
illness or other tragedy. But for those of us with seniors right now, most
likely all are sensing this haze of scariness that has entered and is hovering
above us. It will remain for several weeks, or longer, and then hopefully
leave, without taking our children along.

It's spring. Usually that's a time of incredible joy and promise, and it is
that, too, but those of us with seniors know the sap is running, little rivers
are springing forth with gusto, and our children have cars, and they don't
think they need us anymore.

It's probably even tenser because we remember. We remember the incredible surge to break away that came with that spring. We can almost fully
recall how it felt to be so strong, so invincible, so driven, and so ready to bust
out. We wanted to leave home, leave the rules, leave the control, and go fast.

But we also remember who died in this season. I can still clearly see
the two girls I knew. One crashed on graduation night, and one on prom
night, and neither lived to explain why or how. I know a man who is still in
a nursing home because of a drug he ingested over thirty years ago, on one

senior spring Saturday night. Most of us seem to know someone who did not survive that season of being invulnerable. Many of us know that their parents could never recover.

What I don't know yet is how to shield those who believe they need no shield, who shed or reject the protection, or deceive or outsmart the protector. How do you convince someone with no fear to be cautious?

I know I learned through those who crashed and those who died.

I learned, decades later, how thin is the thread that keeps us here when I was hit head-on by a man in a pick-up truck, who decided that he was straight enough to drive when he was not. I know in my bones how fast it happens. I so know how it feels to know that death is an option, and how it is to depend on that ambulance, those doctors, on one's God, and not on anything the self can do. But, how do you teach that terror to someone who needs to be brave to face the world as an adult?

I don't know how to walk this line any better with Number Five than I did with Number One. I don't know the end of trust, from the beginning of negligence. I don't know the line that separates enough questions from too many. I know I cannot stop worrying, but how much of that worry do I place on his shoulders? Am I arrogant or ignorant to believe he will remember what he has been taught? Does he, or any other senior this spring, have any idea how much they are loved, and needed, and treasured? Do they have any idea what they risk?

I also know that I do not want Dr. Phil, or the other self-righteous guy in the paper, to presume to tell me the exact formula to use to react during this season. Because, after five seniors, I know there is no formula. They are, none of them, alike. What guided one does not necessarily guide another. What one son or daughter learned to value is certainly not replicated by the next one. The conversations are subtle and searching for all involved. Nothing is overt. Nothing is clearly black or white or transparent. We hold on, knowing we are letting go.

Maybe all of us parents, and all who love graduating children, just plain have to become walking prayers during this time of year. Maybe we all wear our hearts hanging humbly, while our heads attempt a last, valiant, hyper-vigilance. Maybe it's a rite of passage and separation for all of us. But, even after five, I still don't know how to do it well, without error. Maybe we can't know. Maybe we're not supposed to know. I hate that part the most.

It's Too Bad about the Bagpipes

We place markers in our lives for many reasons. They signal turning points, new directions, and sometimes important reflections.

I GUESS THERE WAS SUPPOSED TO BE a parade of bagpipes winding its way through the trees on the campus. However, the courtyard was sodden, and the skies were dark and rolling, and we were inside. She graduated, nonetheless.

In this season of graduations and tulips and daffodils and the last claws of winter, we went to the Cities to watch the eldest graduate from college. It was the first college graduation I have ever attended as a member of the audience. I only knew one of the five hundred or so graduates, her roommate, and a small handful of her closest friends.

He said that it is the unknown that pulls us forward, not the known.

So, in that large, overflowing, and enclosed place, I focused by taking notes on the guest speaker. And what a speaker he was! Her college chose a poet, Edward Hirsch, a poet in this day and time, published in myriad print forms, including *The New Yorker* magazine. He spoke of the creative process.

He talked about how the students preparing to graduate now know a lot, but the creative process is not about what they know. It's about what they don't know. It's about realizing that what is known, by all of our kind, becomes insignificant when compared with what is unknown. He said that it is the unknown that pulls us forward, not the known. He told the graduates that it is their future as educated thinkers to add to what is known.

The creative process brings us face-to-face with the unknown and helps us to find an angle to understand what is yet to be understood. Hirsch wished for the graduates vitality and nerve. I heard him tell us that what is most daring and most original in all of us is what we need to nurture and treasure, and I looked at our girl's fragile shoulders in her little gown and remembered the times when none of us "so-called adults" that love her knew what to do, what to expect, how to predict, how to provide for what it was she could become, because she was so daring and so original.

She, and all the beautiful, high-minded, undaunted graduates in her class—in fact, all children, everywhere—are creative acts. They are, all of them, the unknown. They are what pulls us forward, and they are what enables us to see into the future.

Edward Hirsch explained that works of art need nurturing and giant amounts of energy and focus and heart and soul. He told the audience that when the creative process pierces the unknown, a work of art takes on a "majestic inner glow," magic, and strangeness. And then she walked across the stage, glowing, radiant, magical, and newly strange.

In one of his poems, and I searched and searched, unsuccessfully, to find which one, Edward Hirsch talks of being very small on a large beach. So small, so very small, and then, fully aware of his smallness, he asks this question, "How can I be filled with such vast love?"

She accepted her diploma and turned to her best friend since first grade, and her sisters, and she beamed. Her small, tiny self paused on the platform, shooting immense and intense beacons of love far past them and us and into her future, beyond what it is we can now understand.

III. Improving

M Y FIELD, MY SPECIALTY, the theory and application that I teach to university students, is that of assessment— the measurement of learning, and by reflection, the effectiveness of teaching.

Frankly, it's a pretty slippery field.

It's slippery especially because it is hard to measure something that defies definition. We have yet to clearly and uniformly define what it is that we want schools to do, exactly.

We have not agreed upon a set of standards of learning to which we hold all schools and all teachers accountable. That's what makes it nearly impossible to measure success in schools. We don't know what success is.

I, personally, am pretty happy about that. I fear that if it is ever defined, the definition will be too narrow to allow for joy in learning.

Another reason why my field is slippery is because of assembly lines. Because of assembly lines and industry, we have learned, as a particular culture, to measure productivity in numbers. Measurement in numbers is easy. One just counts.

The problem with measuring using numbers in education is that so many things that we value in our children's learning cannot be quantified. So very many things, like compassion, reason, invention, dedication, honesty, interpretation, self-reflection, growth, respect, and even working well with others cannot be measured across large populations using bubble sheets, Number 2 pencils, and normal curves. So, how can we be sure that we are improving?

Recent legislation has asked us to use more and more tests. We are currently using bubble sheets to let parents and other taxpayers know how well schools are doing on bubble sheets. The intent of the legislation was to establish some kind of dialog, some kind of accountability, for the billions of federal dollars aimed at leveling the field for children. We need to be vigilant as to other effects of this measurement as compared to what we value in learning in classrooms where children we care about have desks.

Looking at how we measure learning is a fascinating, rich, and controversial field, alive with possibilities for clear communication and common understandings, for feedback and monitoring, adjustment and progress. We just can't get bogged down in the numbers. There's a lot more to accountability than graphs and charts and bubble sheets.

We've Got to Know Where We Are Going

It's so much easier not to set goals for students or schools.
That way, we never fall short of them. However, without goals,
improvement is random and isolated. We can do better.

MAN, IT IS JUST SO HARD to plan how to get somewhere when we don't know where we are going. I have always understood that form should follow function; that first we decide what we want to do, and then we should find out how best to make sure we do it.

I'm not saying that a random road trip is not fun. It's a treat, sometimes, to just load up the car and see how far we can get, going a particular direction, stopping whenever we see something interesting, and resting a lot. But, it is really almost stupid to pack up and go, knowing we need to be somewhere fast yet having to guess at our destination. It's frustrating to be both urgent and unsure.

I kind of feel that way when making improvement plans for schools. We know we need to show the feds and the state and the district that we have planned well, but our ultimate reason for all this improvement seems to be so illusive sometimes.

Take high schools, for instance.

We can use the test scores from the mandated state testing, the dropout rates, the scores that students receive on college admissions testing, absence and discipline data, grades, and surveys, and we can notice where we may be behind the eight ball and plan to do something about it.

We can work to keep the kids in school more and longer. We can work to ensure that they score higher more often on the state tests that measure math, writing, and reading. We can work to reduce the number of kids that end up suspended. We can try to increase the numbers of students in higher-level courses.

But, how do we know for sure that if more students are in school that they are learning more? Even more problematic, can we promise that if high school students attend, they will have learned what they need to know to make it out there?

Here's some stuff we do know. We know that about 30 percent of those students enrolled in ninth grade are no longer enrolled by graduation—nationwide. We know that the level of reading necessary to succeed in college and the level of reading necessary to succeed in entry-level jobs for those who don't attend college is about the same. We know that some students do a whole lot better in schools that are geared and organized differently than traditional high schools. We think students do better in smaller learning communities. We know that businesses and manufacturers are calling for workers who can be there, follow through, and work hard. We also know that we are scared, as a nation, that we are losing our edge, owing to a lack of talent and knowledge in the fields of math, science, and engineering, and that our students need to learn more Arabic and Chinese. And, to save our planet, what could be more important than introducing the next generation to an awareness of the natural world in which we live?

So, if you ran a high school, what would you do first?

Would you begin with bringing in Chinese language courses, or would you work to bring down the dropout rate? Would you start with increasing math capacity, and if so, in which grades? Would you work to provide increased instruction for students at risk of having trouble finding work at all, or would you put funding at the upper end to create engineers? Would you choose to concentrate on providing courses and opportunities for students to interact with their environment, or would you give them the chance to learn how to work hard, on time, and within deadlines at something that matters to them?

I have always been a firm believer that there is no such thing as a full dishwasher. One can always find room for one more plate, or fork, if needed. However, I do believe there are such things as too many expectations, funding spread too thin, and staffs at the breaking point. We do need to decide what we want and communicate that to our schools.

If we cannot come to agreement, then we need to evolve in the way that TV has in the past couple of decades. We used to have only three channels. Now we have hundreds. Maybe high schools need to become specialized and quit trying to be all for all.

There is a point when the machine, or the institution, can no longer take one more task without blowing up. We are already asking more of our high schools than can be done. We need to stop setting them up to fail no matter how hard they try.

We need to give them a clear destination, so they can arrive.

Lights, Pucks, and Standards

What do standards have to do with anything anyway?
Why do we need to know what students are expected to learn?

THERE ARE, I SUPPOSE, SOME PUPPY DOGS, politicians, and self-righteous seventeen-year-olds who still believe that there are right, easy answers to big questions. There are, of course, easy answers to big questions, but I think that those answers are usually wrong. Easy answers, in my experience, are logical only to those whose understanding is limited. When this limited logic is applied liberally, it usually creates a slippery slope into dark and scary, fearful and threatened positions. If however, light (rather than one-sided logic) is applied liberally, we see the tunnel, the end of the tunnel, and we can even see the opposition legitimately and deal respectfully with it.

So, what does this have to do with schools? Lots. In fact, by watching the oppositions define and redefine what is important in Minnesota's public schools over the past several years, we have weathered the trump and triumph of several forms of logic that have competed in the form of state standards. State standards define what students will be expected to know and to be able to do by attending public schools. State standards define what teachers will be expected to teach in public schools. State standards define the learning that will be tested by tests that will be used to rate the success of public schools.

If everything lines up, if students are taught what they are expected to know and do, and if the tests accurately measure that knowledge, then we will be able to see if schools are successful at doing what they are being asked to do. Simple? Not by a long shot.

The first beam of light on this issue comes in the form of the question, "What is it that schools are being asked to do?" I could go on and on about the added social expectations that have been heaped upon schools in the past ten years alone. Schools check for lice and work on conflict-resolution skills; they provide breakfasts before school and programs after school; they provide for students and families that speak one of eighty or so languages other than English at home; and they open early and stay open late to provide access to computers. Schools find pathways to educate students with a whole spectrum of special needs, and they help to find scholarships for myriad students each year. Schools deal with sexual harassment, racism, gangs, escalating violence, drag racing in the parking lots, and so much more, with shrinking staffs and funding cuts year after year. I'm not even going to scratch the surface of the many issues of social importance that find their ways into the classrooms.

I am going to go to a different place altogether. From a parent's point of view, I have always known that schools are the wombs for the society

From a parent's point of view, I have always known that schools are the wombs for the society we wish to create or to replicate.

we wish to create or to replicate. So, if we want a future without racism, then we need to grow that future in our schools. If we want a future that divides society, then that is what we should see happening in schools. "What kind of world do we want to see in our schools?" is a marvelous, multifaceted, complex question that reflects the values and the vision of the cradling civilization. By defining new programs daily and weekly, and by adding new responsibilities to the creaking foundations of the institutions now in practice, we never really define our expectations clearly for schools. How can they ever, then, really succeed except sometimes, by some standards, for some folk?

So, second beam of light. Second question: "What is it that students are expected to know and do?" This is the question we have answered at our state levels with the creation and adoption of state standards. These standards currently delineate knowledge at each grade level in reading, language arts, writing, math, social studies, science, and more. If you are curious, I urge you to check out the newly adopted standards in our state. They can be found at http://www.education.mn.us.

As a mom, I just can't really care about the line after line of standards. Instead, I wonder if standards offer enough viewpoints to help my children see a large and wonderful world, but frankly, I trust that teachers will always teach more than these bare-bones lists of things.

Here's what I do want. I want all six of my children to leave school knowing the gifts that each of them bring to the world. I want all six of them, regardless of their limitations, to leave school able to make it in this world. I want them to be able to get along; find what they need; recognize beauty, excellence, and baloney; and I want them to be able to find help when they need it. I want them to understand and use math and science creatively and effectively. I want them to be able to communicate well and to learn forever. I want them to be able to solve problems rather than admire and glorify problems. I will teach them about my faith. I will teach them what I value. I want the schools to teach them how to navigate in a world that I will not see.

How is a simple multiple-choice test going to measure how successful a school is at doing what I want it to do?

It has been said that we value what we measure, and we measure what we value. I cannot, as a mom, value what is in the state standards enough to assign success or failure to schools based upon tests that measure only those standards.

I question the validity of the instruments, the validity of what is measured, and even the possibility of creating a standing list of what is important in so complex an institution. Learning is about being and becoming. It's so not simple.

Therefore, although the tests my children have been taking for the past couple of months could prove helpful in raising questions of equity and practices, I cannot see them as helpful in giving me much of a picture as to whether my own kids have learned what I want them to learn, or what I want schools to teach. For that information, I don't know where to turn exactly. I wish I did.

For a long time now, I think my favorite educational philosopher has been the great hockey player Wayne Gretzky. He was once asked how it is that he always skates to where the puck is. His reply was that he never skates to where the puck is, he skates to where it's going to be.

When a child enters school, the system is aiming toward a goal at least twelve years into the future. The world, twelve years from now, will be far removed from the present. Therefore, I do wish that we would turn our lights toward that future with our standards, our testing, and our evaluations. If we did, then I would guess we would focus on a bigger picture for our kids, complete with complex skills, thought processes, and ideas. We wouldn't focus on that which is easy to measure; instead, we would focus on that which really counts.

And what counts needs to count for all of us. Children in Duluth will be attending kindergarten roundup this week. Our success with them sits out there thirteen years from now. It's not too soon to flip on the lights, throw out that puck, and begin to move it gracefully on that slippery surface, past skilled player after skilled player, toward an agreed-upon goal. The net, of course, needs to be constructed by all of us who love our children, and the game, and those who sharpen our aim.

On Deciding Who's Above Average

Is it unnatural to let everyone have a chance to win?

I SUPPOSE THERE JUST HAS TO BE a group of winners, and there has to be a group of losers. It would be unnatural, I imagine, if we structured the Super Bowl, or the Olympics, so that everyone could win. I guess it would be too strange if we set the bar at a flawless performance on figure skates, or a yet-unheard-of time on the grand slalom, or even a number of successful shots at the goal in hockey, and then whoever or whatever team attained the stated goals would win the gold medal.

If that were the case, then it would be possible for all competitors to attain a prize. It would also be possible that no one would attain a prize. I know, I know—it's not going to happen. But I wonder how we would be different, all of us, if we didn't compete against one another and instead competed against a standard worth attaining? The standard could rise as its conquerors multiplied, but the goal would be the thing, not the smashing of opponents, or the establishment of a class of losers as an inevitable by-product of the identification of winners.

My master's-level students are struggling with this question as applied to students in schools. If we have A's, do we also absolutely need D's and F's? Is the creation of a curve a necessary part of school? What happens if we establish a goal and set our students up to challenge the goal itself, without consideration of rank, effort, or a normal curve?

For instance, just say we set a goal that all students in a particular program must be able to change a tire on a midsize car, make breakfast for ten, create a scatter plot to illustrate a correlation, set up experiments that accurately determine the composition of a chemical solution, and analyze the television show *Lost* to correctly identify the hero, the antihero, and the tragic hero. If any student does all of the above, the reward is an A for the course. It's possible that all of the students could receive A's, and it's also possible that no one would.

The thing about ranking in schools, if we look at patterns, is that the same people always seem to be on top. I once asked a veteran kindergarten teacher if she could tell which of her little ones were going to excel as high school students. She said her predictions were about 100 percent accurate. I asked her how long it took her, how many months did she need to interact with her darling innocents before she could make accurate predictions? She told me that it took her about two weeks.

By establishing a curve, structuring tests and assignments to always rank, it seems we reinforce the predictions from kindergarten over and over again. I wonder how long it takes for a child to see in the mirror what the kindergarten teacher sees in two weeks? How many rankings does it take before a child labels himself or herself as a loser or a winner?

I know that, to some, life is about competition. I know that there is a thrill in winning and a lesson in loss. Please know that I am not going to the extreme of suggesting that we eliminate the crowning of champions. Instead, I am just thinking about trying something different in classrooms when it is appropriate. I am just wondering if we could give more options, more often, when each student has the chance to grasp the gold without fear of there not being enough room on the platform. If we set a bar, and they all get there, is that a bad thing?

I have watched my own children compete over and over again. Sometimes they have been winners. Sometimes they have not. I have watched them become elated at the A's, the recognitions. I have also watched them pack little dreams in dark, locked boxes and close doors to involvement forever, due to low grades and a lack of encouragement, knowing that they never ranked above average.

So, my questions and challenges are these: What is average, anyway? Why do we need to know? Who decides, and on what basis? Our society has, for decades, looked to our schools to produce workers, managers, leaders, and followers. I just wonder why we keep students for twelve years if we know in kindergarten which students are bound for glory and which are not. I wonder what would happen if we opened the gate wide and assumed that all are above average, with limitless capacity. What would happen if schools were not asked to sort and instead were given the mandate to set the bar and provide the means to get there?

What if we gave every learner the chance to grab that brass ring more often? There's room. Their hands are small.

'Tis the Season

··

*This is not about holidays. This is about the time of year when teachers
and schools gear up for the annual mandated test days. Mandated tests are
relatively new in our schools, and there are high stakes attached to the results.*

IT'S TESTING SEASON. I would imagine that if you are not involved
in one way or another with public schools, Testing Season passes by as
an unremarkable, inconsequential poof on the horizon. If you work in,
or attend, a public elementary or secondary school, Testing Season is
probably a big, darn deal.

Testing Season is not a jolly season. The actual testing window, the
period of time when students are led to rooms with desks and tables and
Number 2 pencils, begins in April and continues until May. From my
observations, in just about the middle of February, in schools across this
state, the preparation begins in earnest. Although many teachers may have
been preparing students all year, now is the time when concentrated full-
bore test preparation goes into full swing. Students practice taking tests.
They practice filling in bubble sheets. They self-correct, peer-correct, and
then turn in final drafts of practice writings, practice solutions of math
problems, and practice answers demonstrating comprehension of complex
passages.

Schools send cards to homes in Testing Season, with pleas and
supplications to make sure that first, students actually arrive on testing
day, and second, that they come prepared to gear up and take tests
conscientiously.

It's just that so much rides on those few days.

So much depends on attendance and scores that these testing days
have become either days of doom or days when doom is thwarted once

again—one or the other. Doom, of course, would be delivered in the sanctions that are part of the No Child Left Behind Act.

NCLB is not a Minnesota deal, although the students in our schools will be taking tests that measure their progress against Minnesota Standards. No Child Left Behind is a federal deal. It is the law that governs the distribution of federal dollars earmarked for programs to level the playing field for children. No Child Left Behind provides funding for Head Start and for other programs serving English language learners, home-

So much rides on these...few weeks. Funding, levels of interference, public perception, and more depend on what happens on desks with Number 2 pencils.

less children, and children who are at risk for failure due to many factors. In Minnesota schools, those funds are massive.

The law requires that we test all of our students in several grades against state standards in the subjects of math, language arts, and science. So, we do.

The law requires that we have almost every single child present, accounted for, and tested, so we call parents of students who have not been in school (in some cases for months) and impress upon them the importance, the urgency, of having the students show up on testing day.

The law requires that we place the scores our students earn during Testing Season into categories and that we report those scores to the public. So, we do.

The No Child Left Behind Act has declared its goal to be that children in America will attain scores considered "proficient" by the year 2014. That means, in each subgroup, children will test and pass at a predetermined level. Subgroups under this law include groups of children qualified to receive special education services and groups of children categorized by ethnicity, eligibility for free or reduced-cost lunch, gender, and even a category of students who have been in the district for less than one year. Each and every group is expected to show its members as proficient by the year 2014.

In order to make sure that each group in each school is moving at a pace that will permit proficiency to happen, schools are assigned, each year for each subgroup, a target score. That score is called "Adequate Yearly Progress," and if any subgroup in any Title I school fails to make Adequate Yearly Progress for two years in a row, that school publicly enters "Needs Improvement" status, and things get serious, indeed. Oh, and if any subgroup does not have almost every single student tested, the school will enter sanction status no matter what the scores reveal.

So much rides on these next few weeks. Funding, levels of interference, public perception, and more depend on what happens on desks with Number 2 pencils. The tests take hours. The results mark years to come.

The question of whether we can measure the worth of a school in a single set of tests is not the point. Neither is the question of whether we value measurement in math, science, and language arts more than we value measurement in the arts, health, fitness, citizenship, social awareness, or myriad other capacities. The question during Testing Season of whether we believe in what we are measured against is not the point at all.

The point is that it's time to test, and so we do. And we cross our fingers in hopes that we will awaken after Testing Day and find no lumps of coal under our trees of knowledge, and no big, ugly rocks stuffed in the hanging stockings that hold our students' hopes for their futures.

Data That Matta

....

*Numbers are neutral. Even a whole lot of numbers are meaningless
unless we decide they matter.*

THE SCORES ARE UP. Acres and acres of data are being prepared, as
I write this, to be sent out to the public, about how our schools did on
a series of tests required by our state's interpretation of the federal No
Child Left Behind Act. Spreadsheet after spreadsheet, graph after graph,
field after field, a veritable forest of facts, should hit the papers this week,
and then we'll know.

So, here's what I feel compelled to state as the inundation begins: "Dang.
I wish it wasn't done this way."

The thing is, data itself is neutral. Alone, a test score really can't mean
anything. Even acres and acres of test scores don't mean a thing unless we
say they do. We ascribe meaning to the numbers. The numbers themselves
cannot tell us anything at all unless we let them.

They do make for good news. One thing for sure about numbers
is that they make clean and colorful and controversial copy. Numbers
enable rankings and comparisons. They make it easy to point fingers. They
make it possible to reduce complex systems that serve intricate, delicate,
impressionable young minds to simple shorthand.

But, just because numbers can make simplification possible doesn't
mean that they mean what folks may think they mean. Just because we can
doesn't mean that we should use them to describe schools.

So, before we take seriously the ascribed meaning assigned to the test
scores that are used to label schools as either "fine" or "underperforming," I
so hope we consider a few things.

Like, for instance, the fact that the scores you will see online, or in the
paper, and everywhere else are the scores attained last year, by the students
in our schools last year. The third graders last year are in fourth grade now,
pretty much. No matter what, we probably most likely won't put them back
in third grade, teach them differently, and have them take the test again. We

don't know how this year's third graders would have done taking the same test. In other words, we are receiving information that may or may not be helpful to the students who will take the tests later this year. We are making cross-cohort generalizations, and that's not particularly precise.

Of course, if we had hundreds and hundreds of students in a school at a particular grade level, we could possibly read trends or something into the scores. But, man oh man, if we have twenty or thirty or even one hundred students in a grade level in a school, the presence or absence of even five students can skew the scores significantly. If two sets of twins and a random child moved out, or moved in, we could have had a whole different set of results in a whole lot of places.

Frankly, I'm just getting warmed up. Here's another thing to think about. The data, the raw test scores or the scaled test scores, cannot reflect the mission, vision, or beliefs of the people behind the labels. Numbers only indicate how a set of students responded to a set of questions on a given day.

Some high schools in this state are located in places where living can seem harsh. The doors of these schools are open to students who have dropped out of other schools, perhaps because they just could not connect to the structure, the staff, or the expectations. Those schools are founded and dedicated to serving students in innovative ways, by organizing learning differently, being open different hours, offering connections to culture, or work, or finding ways to help those who have fallen too far behind to find faith in themselves and the means to catch up. Their students come with giant invisible backpacks of failure and disenfranchisement. Some of them come in the fall, and others come whenever they decide to try again. Yet, these students take the tests on the same day as everyone else.

Is it any surprise that the scores from schools dedicated to trying to turn lives around show students lacking in skills? Those schools provide hope and success for students who feel as if they were thrown away. How then can the numbers generated by the test scores serve to label those places as underperforming? How can it possibly be true that those places may have to face closure because their test scores reflect the fact that they serve students who are willing to try again after years of being left behind?

We will see numbers. We just have to be careful what else we see, and through whose eyes, and we need to keep in mind that the numbers cannot tell a story. For that, we need to ask a lot more questions of the people in the places, and then we need to listen. Then we need to care.

Grades, Effort, and
Packing the Horn Away

*What does a grade mean, anyway? Why is it that we put value on a letter
grade without knowing how it was attained?*

I AM SO SICK OF GRADES. Grades are what my children bring home
that indicate…what, exactly? For some teachers, the grade is affected by the
number of tardies, whether work was turned in late, as well as whether the
child understood the deeper levels of information presented and examined.
For some teachers, the grade is only a reflection of achievement toward
learning objectives. For others, it seems the grade is an indicator of the space
between perceived ability
and perceived engagement
of that ability. Yet others
assign grades based on effort.
What exactly does effort look
like across cultures, across
economics, even across
personalities? I do have a hard time helping my children when I cannot
explain the basis upon which the grade stands.

*What exactly does effort look like
across cultures, across economics,
even across personalities?*

One of my children tells me that he pays a classmate to put his horn
away after band class so that he can dash out of the room, across the
building, and make it to his next class on time. Why? Because, if he is late,
his grade will go down fast. He can figure out no other way. So, is his grade
an indication of his ability to pay a tuba-sitter?

The pressure is so very there. I have just been part of a long discussion regarding high school honors courses and grades given in honors
courses. It seems there are some students who do not choose honors

104 JULES ON SCHOOLS

classes because the grades are more difficult to attain, and those students want to keep their GPAs high, so they don't sign up. Man!

Grades get so icky! I have watched my daughters spend so much time in states of anxiety over one grade or another for their entire educational careers and counting! I watched my sons spend just as much time baffled over the whys and hows involved with grade getting. I have also watched five of them, attending five different colleges, struggle to work through whole new sets of "Rules for Grade Getting."

And so, what do you call an engineer, or a teacher, or a geographer, or a surgeon who received mostly "C's" in their professional course work? You call them engineers, teachers, geographers, and surgeons. The grades stop counting once the formal schooling ends.

I realize that grades are gatekeepers. They belong to a class of data that some would label "common metrics." Common metrics are measurements that people believe mean something, like certain test scores, or yardsticks, or home run averages. The truth is, any measurement is neutral until we assign meaning to it. The "A" carries no power, unless we ascribe power to it. We have assigned so much power to a letter grade that has no definitive definition. We have given so much weight to a letter that means something different to almost every single dispenser of that grade. Everyone knows that an "A" means excellent, right? But excellent in what regard? It gets even messier when it comes to "B's." Does a "B" mean that my child doesn't quite understand; or that he turned everything in late; or that he gets it, but he was too obnoxious; or that he understands the lessons, but he couldn't pay the rising tuba-tender prices?

In order for students to be eligible for a number of scholarships, a student must be in the top 10 percent of the class. Fair enough, except that to be in the top 10 percent means a student must receive only very, very good grades. So, if a student registers for an honors class and receives a "B," which lowers the GPA, that student's exposure to advanced learning may place the scholarship in jeopardy.

What are we teaching our children? Well, there's strategy, of course. There's guessing our way around the system. There's going after the prize no matter what, and certainly, there's the lesson about taking the path of less resistance because that will make all the difference. All of these are very important lessons, indeed. They must be, since they are reinforced so predictably.

There must be a better way. There must be a way to minimize the impact, or even stop the impact, of the grade in order to clear a path to valuing learning for its own sake. There must be a better means to communicate the student's level of learning to those who make decisions based on that level of achievement. There is, however, not an easy way. There is no other common metric out there with as much mileage or as much misplaced, but massive, credibility. I cannot see grades fading away fast.

I would, however, challenge those who award scholarships to look again at the lessons the competition generates and question qualification based on grades alone. Labeling individuals is always playing dangerous language games. Labeling always creates arbitrary, unnatural categories that do not stand up under scrutiny. To label a child as an "A" or a "B" or a "C" or a "D" student is to place that child in a category of persons with very blurry borders that can change arbitrarily and capriciously. To award anything based on GPA is to award…what, exactly, again?

Pain, Enlightenment, and New Mats

....

I'll admit that I so wish effort was enough, and that it worked faster at times.

EFFORT, I HAVE FOUND, is simply both overrated and underappreciated simultaneously.

Currently, as my poor, frayed, and screaming thigh, arm, and ab muscles complain angrily regarding my latest attempts to first find them and then make them work, I really want to see some merit in giving credit for effort.

I have committed, along with a wonderful friend, to fight, once again, the seemingly inevitable slide to amorphousness—to address the fact that our muscles are not visible.

So, we are taking Pilates on Mondays, Yoga on Tuesdays, and Belly Dancing on Wednesdays. That ought to do it.

We bought mats. We paid for the classes. We ride together. And, we are pathetic together.

Our legs shake and quake in Pilates, and the darling, little twenty-year-old instructor chirps, "Just hang in there, we are halfway through!" Our arms are slipping out of their sockets, and our necks are on backwards in Yoga, and the kind, so balanced, mellow, and mellifluous saint who leads us whispers, "Listen to your bodies, and try for a new sensation." In Belly Dance, we shift our hips and find muscles under our ribs that no one ever put there, and our teacher cautions, "This may feel strange to you at first...."

I'm thinking that I deserve some credit for this effort, and some chocolate, and some money.

But no, that's not how it works at all. In the real world, the world outside of Pilates, Yoga, and Belly Dancing, no one can tell by looking at me that I am engaging in effort. My smaller jeans don't just decide to fit because I am trying hard. My scale is not responding fast enough to show any consideration for effort. And, as of tonight, my abs, thighs, butt, and arm muscles hurt, but they still jiggle. Dang!

The thing is, effort is so darn subjective. It really doesn't show, or even look the same, on any of us. I think an hour a day is pretty impressive. However, my son who plays basketball far away from here rises at 5 a.m., lifts weights and conditions for three hours, goes to classes, then trains for three more hours, and then plays pickup ball in the gym all evening long. My effort looks pretty puny in comparison.

So, how does effort fit into the training or learning process? As a parent and as a student, I have been warned of lack of effort, begged for a bit more effort, and praised for "just such inspiring effort."

Can we define clearly what effort looks like? Can we, as teachers or as learners, clearly describe what effort looks like across gender, cultures, social mores, and developmental levels? Is effort in intent, or in performance? Is there a definite line between effort, futility, and self-preservation? At what point does effort become stubbornness, stupidity, or just currying favor?

In the world outside of schools and classrooms, what does effort earn? Will the team choose the athlete who practices hardest or the one who can run and hit the hardest? Will the CEO reward the worker who stays the longest or the one who brings in the biggest sales? Do we want to watch the ballerina who sweats the most, or the one who makes the impossible look sublime?

Right now, I want some kudos for my efforts. I want some credit for the fact that it takes six minutes for me to stand up because of the knots and protests. I want a pat on the back (gently), and a kiss on the forehead. But it does stop there. I am not asking for a reward in cash or anything.

After all these years in schools, I do believe that rewarding effort is a very slippery slope. Effort can take too many forms to be readily recognized. It can look like nothing at all, and it can often be feigned. Plus, rewarding and recognizing effort gives a false picture of the world the student faces outside the classroom.

In the end, it doesn't matter if I love or hate the Pilates, Belly Dancing, or Yoga; whether I sweat, or burn, or pitch a fit. What matters is whether I can lead a balanced and disciplined life, or not. The proof of that will not be in the purchase of the mat, the attendance at the classes, or in the number of times I complain. It will be in the life I lead and the energy that surrounds me. For some learners, that prize comes naturally and easily, through grace or genetics, but for the rest of us, it probably takes some pretty focused effort over time, some BENGAY, and a little self-pity. The reward remains the same, however, regardless of the price paid or the perception of the price paid. And in the big picture, that may well be more fair than we can know, from where we stand now.

We All Have Tests

How did we educators let something as elegant as a conversation between the teacher and the learner morph into the punishment that tests have become?

I CANNOT EVEN GET MY HEAD AROUND THE LOGIC of it, let alone the ethics. I find myself just pursing my lips and shaking my head, and even doing a little shudder. I am sure anyone watching me must think I have become doddering. Maybe I have.

My eldest son called this weekend. He was stressed out, again. He is studying to become an engineer, and his courses have sounded impossible to me for years. He stresses mostly over tests. He and his band of calculator-carrying friends study all the time. OK, sometimes with libation, but they are incredibly dedicated. They have seen their numbers dwindle, and in this final, unending homestretch, there are only a few remaining with the eye still on the prize. Yet, he carries fear on his shoulders. They all do. Over tests.

This time, his professor had told them to study a specified number of chapters. They did. Then, on the test, the questions came from the next set of chapters. They did their best. Sometimes, my son's tests come from material not covered, and other times they do. He never knows.

If his school were the only place where that happened, I wouldn't be so frustrated. It's not. I have a different son who recently failed a test that did not ask any questions about the assignments or the readings; instead, it asked obscure questions about the captions under the pictures. I remember my daughter calling every single classmate she knew to get help understanding a theory they had all heard in class (because the test was in the morning), and not one could help her. The whole class failed the test, and the scores brought down the grades of all in the room. I hear stories of tests set up to trick the students, to catch them unprepared, to freeze and memorialize a moment of uncertainty. One of my children has a teacher who penalizes for guessing, to the point that some students fear writing what they think they know at all. How sick is that?

I teach assessment at a university. That certainly doesn't make me know more than others about it, but I can surely say I have thought about assessment a lot. And, I have read about it, a lot. After all the reading, thinking, teaching, and reflecting that I have done, I believe I know two things:

1. Learning is a natural act.
2. Assessment is an act of trust.

Assessment, for educators at least, means the measurement of learner mastery. It is the feedback that tells the learner whether he or she has learned, and it tells the teacher whether the class learned and to what degree. It's really that simple. Assessment expert Richard Stiggins and his coauthors (2004) separate the measurements that teachers use into two categories: assessments *for* learning and assessments *of* learning. Teachers who measure students to see how they are doing in order to teach differently if need be, or to see if the class is ready to move on, are doing assessment *for* learning. Teachers who measure to make a judgment and let the students know how they did at the end are doing assessment *of* learning.

> *We are born learners.*
> *If we weren't,*
> *we wouldn't have progressed*
> *much beyond the crib.*

Stiggins says that if students know where they are expected to go and where they are currently, the learning increases more dramatically than with any other factor. Just making sure the student knows what is expected, and how far that student needs to go to get there, can make a huge difference.

So, what is the point of tests that are "gotchas" or that separate the caption readers from the ones who concentrated on the concepts?

We are born learners. If we weren't, we wouldn't have progressed much beyond the crib. It takes a lot to smother and squelch the instinctive desire to learn right out of a child, but we manage.

Assessment, according to theorist and researcher Grant Wiggins (1998, 17), is a moral matter. Deciding what to test (and how to measure it) reveals something about the teacher. It can't help it. Perhaps sending students to a place of fear is good training for something. Perhaps not letting the learner or anyone else in on the expectations is helping them get ready for the "real world" of nasty bosses somewhere.

But, here's the thing. The world of business won't put up with those nasty bosses because their workers are not as productive as those with bosses who set clear expectations. Duh!

Maybe forcing students to take impossible tests makes sure that there are not too many engineers, or whatever—God forbid. Who knows?

Success, like love, has infinite capacity. Punishment, like anger, should be just and limited. Every time a student receives a grade on a test, it becomes part of that learner's self-concept. It's hard to watch a child's self-concept being built based upon judgments from secret places by those who have yet to justify their use of power to the learner, and perhaps to themselves as well.

PIPs and Big Planets and Problems

....

Accountability in the world outside of schools and accountability in the world inside of schools do not, and perhaps should not, share the same criteria.

TODAY, TWO WORLDS COLLIDED right in front of my eyes. Smash! Bang! Bam! Powee! There was dust and fallout and confusion and conflagration for about a nanosecond, and then the bigger world just started spinning again and resumed orbit. The smaller world was left damaged, confused, and begging for understanding.

I began my day today by reading a couple of chapters in Phillip C. Schlechty's book *Working on the Work* (2002). There was a time in my life when I used to begin my days with meditation and inspirational readings, but these days I read, eat, and breathe educational theory exclusively 24/7, or more if I can squeeze it in.

This morning, my trusty yellow highlighter was applied to the following thoughts that Schlechty offered to superintendents, "Until community leaders have a deeper understanding of issues that schools must confront, the strategies they recommend will be informed more by ignorance and passion than by facts and commitments. Thus, educating the community, especially community leaders, about the conditions of education is a necessary antecedent to any meaningful move toward strategic planning" (81).

For the sake of my opening collision metaphor, let's just call the world of education Planet #1—The Small Planet.

Looming on the horizon, replete with resources, power, and the capacity to destroy, would be the larger planet, the world of business and industry, Planet #2—The Death Star Planet.

I attended a "session" in Minneapolis today, on my own dime, advertised as meant for leaders in business, design, and education who aim to improve performance. This "session" featured an expert in Performance Improvement Potential (PIP). As it turned out, I was the only one of my kind in the room. And, it wasn't long before they all knew it.

The expert first dazzled us and then announced that there exists a simple calculation, based on the work of someone named Gilbert (1996), to determine, mathematically, a measurement of opportunity. "Gosh," I thought excitedly, "Could it be as simple as that? Could human potential, the essence of opportunity, be calculated?" I could hardly bear the anticipation.

The expert told us to first *find the exemplar.* This means that in a factory, for instance, a leader must first find the worker who produces the most.

I raised my hand and was acknowledged. "How do we know what that means?" I said. "How do we measure production? Do we use progress, test scores, moral decisions, skill levels, whole class improvement, individual

"We don't have widgets. We have children. They can't become product. We cannot submit all children to the same processes and get the same results."

student baseline-to-target movement, or over time, do we measure each student's net worth? Should we factor in incarceration, ability to adjust, ability to think, to continue to learn, or should we just use multiple choice?"

The expert popped up a graphic on the great screen on the front wall and disdainfully replied, "Well, teacher, you need to choose a unit of measurement and stick with it, and call it a 'widget,' just like we do. Whatever you choose to measure, the formula for Performance Improvement Potential (PIP) = Widgets Produced by Exemplar divided by Average Widget Production. A PIP of 1 means little opportunity, whereas a PIP of 4 to 10 means larger possibilities. Your next step is to analyze the gap between average and exemplar performance and multiply it by the profit per widget. Finally, your calculations should include the potential return on your investment in relationship to your PIP."

Gasps went up from the group. It was all so elegant to them all.

I raised my hand for the last time. "But, Dr. Expert," I said, remembering the advice of Schlechty to communicate the complexities and the real conditions, "We don't have widgets. We have children. They can't become product. We cannot submit all children to the same processes and get the same results. We can't measure 'kid-gets.' We can't even agree as to what constitutes a desired result that is worth measuring, let alone whether we can measure it accurately once we all agree."

"That, teacher, is what is wrong with your whole system," summarized the expert. "That is why we have lost trust in public schools. You have no accountability, no bottom line. You can't seem to see your work as a system of performance."

The session was finally over, and on my way out, a spectacularly suited businessman placed his hand on my inexpensive shoulder and said, "It seemed to me you got kind of beat-up in there. How did it feel to you?"

I stepped on to the elevator and turned to him and said, "Normal. It felt normal to me."

Laundry, the Afterlife, and Evaluations

Who decides if we do things well?

THE GIANT LAUNDRY BASKET CAME HOME this weekend.

He is six feet, eight inches tall, and the dirty laundry was taller. He dumped it and went immediately foraging for food. I did ask him to take the mountain to the laundry room, so that I could better serve him, but it never, ever dawned on me that I should not wash his collegiate collection of smelly sweats, sock balls, raggedy jeans, and statement shirts.

If I would have laughed and let him know that I am not his servant, or if I would have told him how tired I was, or even if I would have delineated my new expectations of a young, independent guy who used to live here, it wouldn't have mattered. I did the laundry, and I lovingly folded each item and matched his socks, partly because I miss him, but mostly because the expectations of momminess in my world include laundry for college sons. It was expected of my mother, and of her mother before her. And if I were to have disturbed that inherited ruling, I would have felt inadequate, less than that which my family deserved, continuing to live knowing for sure that I would have trouble facing my evaluation in the sky as a mother.

We all face evaluations. Some wait until after death, but others happen regularly.

As a professional, I face them every year. Evaluation of teachers in many schools is a formal process, based on observations of actual teaching by a designated supervisor—most often the principal. These days, principals regularly use instruments designed to break teaching into components, such as management, planning, relationships, professional growth, communication, and others. The instruments allow for efficient feedback to teachers who are struggling to improve and who are anxious to know where they stand. In my own situation, we are evaluated on our teaching, our service, and our research—with pretty clear sets of expectations established systemwide.

I know I am lucky. In my situation, I trust and admire those who will evaluate me as a professional. This is not true for all teachers. I cannot imagine the terror of being evaluated by a supervisor who you believe is out to get you. It seems to me that the criteria against which my performance will be judged are transparent—there are no hidden, secret, obscure rules. I also know that this is not always the case for all teachers.

Evaluation is scary for professionals no matter what. When it is clinical, conducted through a series of objective, documented observations, it is probably fair. Yet there are those who would argue that what we do as teachers is more of an art than a science and that what can be observed at specific points in time does not provide a very holistic picture of the teacher at all.

I believe that the scales, instruments, and criteria upon which we are judged have been created with integrity and pure intentions. In the same way, I believe that the expectations of being a mom have been handed down generation after generation with love and good will. I also believe that the even larger sets of expectations that we try to live by, the sets that were given to us through our faiths, were provided to make life better and more rewarding, and they should probably not be revisited, usually.

However, the other sets, the expectations of us as parents or professional educators are not so written in stone. They should be open to challenge and revision.

Some schools use new and innovative methods of evaluation, dependent on the goals of each individual educator. There are places that use a clinical model for the first years and then allow teachers to evaluate themselves in consultation with their peers and to be judged based on personal professional goals and the attainment of those goals.

The truth is, we don't always need to do things the way they have always been done. We don't need to judge ourselves or one another based on scales, instruments, or generational understandings after they have become outdated and uninformative.

We need to question whether laundry really makes a difference in the big picture, just as we need to wonder whether it matters if we always use an anticipatory set in lessons.

The ancient poet Rumi advised us to sell our cleverness and buy bewilderment. What if we did? What would happen if we worked hard to determine our own set of expectations and then found the means to live up to them? Just what do you think would really happen if we committed to always getting better at what we do, and then we did?

Separating the Ballou from the Ballyhoo

....

We do remarkable things as teachers. Mostly, what we do is relatively
unnoticed and uncelebrated. When one of us is recognized, that recognition
can serve to remind us all to think about how we teach school.

IN THE MIDST OF SCHOOL CONSOLIDATION PROPOSALS, the end-
of-the-year activities when everything is due, the worry about budget and
programming cuts and whether all teachers will retain their jobs next year,
and in the middle of wondering about what will happen to our children in
our schools, sometimes we do need to sit still and listen. My mother always
told me that the voice of what is right is small. She told me that if we are to
hear the right stuff, we need to still the shrill sounds of worry, frustration,
and anger, and we need to wait. We need to pay attention to who performs
the miracles without the banners and rallies. We need to differentiate the
systems from what makes the systems work.

So, in the middle of everything chaotic last week, my wonderful,
quiet, humble friend shyly smiled at me as we recovered from our Yoga
class over a dinner of nondescript chicken and told me in one sentence
that her principal had nominated her for an award and that she had won.
My friend Jane Ballou teaches students ranging from eighth graders to
seniors at the Secondary Technical Center (STC), which is part of Duluth
Public Schools and is located on the hill next to Central High School.
This year, she is Minnesota's Vocational Educator of the Year.

On paper, Jane teaches her learners how to work "the front of
the house" in food services, and how to organize catering and run
delicatessens. Many of her waiter/waitress students come to her too
shy to look up from their notepads, their voices so shaky their words
are imperceptible, their ability to organize remote at best. They leave
confident, with an organizational schema capable of impressive

multitasking while appearing graceful and gracious. They leave with poise and capacity.

Jane's catering students learn to prioritize, listen to consumers, gauge a market, and perform under pressure. They learn to price items and seek profit reasonably. They learn the value of appearance, aesthetics, innovation, and uniform production. They learn how to appreciate subtle variation. They learn a lot about class.

Students in her Deli class learn how to market, respond, pilot and test products, and they learn how to sell and display foods. They learn about the effects of quality on profit and loss, and they begin to sense the interaction between customers and service. They learn to work in teams and to parse production. They learn to respect whom they serve.

Of course, they all learn a lot more than that, too. They learn by watching their teacher as she works outside of her job to raise funds to take them on field trips to wonderful restaurants and to our nation's largest food show in Chicago. They watch her as she sets clear guidelines, and as she finds a way to make each of them successful, no matter what. They watch her treat them with love, kindness, and respect, and they see that she expects the same in return when they work with her and with one another.

Jane's students employ knives, ovens, slicers, and flame, and they watch her carefully instill a competence for each tool in each of them. Her students learn about the importance of sanitation and maintaining high standards, and she will not allow for violation of those standards. Her students learn about being on time, working very hard, and never letting down those who depend on them.

Under the disguise of learning about food service, Jane's students learn about being adults who contribute. They also learn about being adults who teach and adults who care.

In his recommendation for this year's award, STC Principal Jim Arndt referred to Jane's understanding of the child as a whole person. He spoke of how Jane not only spends many, many evenings a year at her students' volleyball, basketball, football, soccer, and track events, but that she follows the teams' statistics and then speaks to her students about their standings and upcoming contests. He talked about her mission to seek out some way to let each student feel important, full of potential, and worthy of faith and promise.

I know that a lot of teachers in a lot of schools do the same things, with the same spirit, as does my friend Jane. I wish that all could receive even a parcel of the recognition deserved.

I also know that teachers like Jane do not seek that recognition for work they do so willingly and with such commitment. I know that their reward is not defined by ceremony.

One sunny day last year, after visiting STC for some event, I walked down the sidewalk to the parking lot. Because we are similar in appearance, a student came running from a bus thinking I was her teacher. "Mrs. Ballou," she bubbled and waved, "I'm back! I knew you would be glad to see me!" As she drew closer, she realized that I was not Jane. For that brief instant, however, I felt Jane's real reward by proxy. I saw unbridled joy passed from a student who is known to the teacher who took the time to see and know her, and to care deeply.

IV.
MAKING DECISIONS
ABOUT SCHOOLS

COMPLEX SYSTEMS RARELY FIND simple solutions. On any given day in our schools, we could offer millions of possible answers to the hundreds of questions asked, but the questions and the answers could change the next minute, or at some future time, unexpectedly.

Each day in our schools, we attempt to teach children information to prepare them for lives we can only imagine. Each day, we make our best guesses as to what it is that they will need to know and be able to do to survive and to thrive in a future we will not see.

We cannot see what the technology might be when this year's third graders are thirty.

We cannot know what parts of our culture will remind them of the values that make us great. We cannot know what parts of other cultures should replace the parts of our own taught now, or which should accompany, complement, or contrast with our current philosophies. We don't know what information will free the next generation or what will stifle their possibilities.

We don't know whether they will need to be able to drive a car; choose nutritious foods; write well; sing; speak English, Chinese or Urdu; think logically according to some models, think intuitively according to others, or think critically at all.

We don't know if the way we are teaching today is the best way to serve the needs of children who come to us from so many places, with so many experiences, and so many dreams.

We don't know what we are teaching future citizens by failing to teach them certain things. We are unaware of the effects that might happen if only few or some students read literature from Japan, and others do not. We don't even know the scope of the information we have not chosen to include in our curricula, and the lessons we teach that are not part of our curricula.

Schools and schoolteachers make decisions every day to include or not include, to model behaviors and systems that may be strange to some and familiar to others. Teachers every day in each classroom teach from books, from the world around them, and from their hearts. They transmit knowledge and values simultaneously and are sometimes unaware of the subtle lessons their actions teach well.

Teachers provide lenses and mirrors for the children in their care, and schools are the vessels for infinite lessons in every minute. Today's children will in turn transmit those lessons infinitely into the future.

There are no simple answers, no easy formulas.

Schools are places where life happens abundantly.

Spitting Downtown and Paying Attention

....

What happens in the halls of our houses and senates is our business.

THERE ARE THOSE WHO SAY THAT SCHOOLS are removed from politics, that once you enter the schoolhouse door, politics are no longer relevant. They say that learning is not a political act.

Except, it is.

My first job of teaching English was located within spitting distance of our state capitol. Yet I spent my first years paying absolutely no attention to what was happening downtown. I saw no connection between what I did with my dear, dear children in my own classroom and the sausage making that happened in the legislature. I did not want to believe that individuals who had never taught for one day in their lives had so much control over children and teachers in schools.

But, I grew up.

As I grew up, I came to realize things about politics and schools. First, I learned that anyone who ever went to school has something to say about what schools should do and how they should be run. Second, because of our political systems in this country, we have created the most glorious system of public education, but depending on who is in charge, that institution can serve to maintain the status quo, or it can be used as the most powerful instrument of social change ever envisioned. Depending on politics and power, some, all, or none of our children will have access to some, all, or none of the ideas that will serve as the basis for the thinking of the future.

I have come to understand that if we believe that what happens in Saint Paul stays in Saint Paul, then we are part of the problem. If you are in schools, it is hard not to see the problems that classrooms reflect every single day.

Every day, there are children in classrooms who are afraid, ashamed, anemic, or anxious beyond the sum of their years. Every day, we see the same groups of students succeed, and the same groups of students lose, by and large. Every day, we watch what we do become more and more reduced to a series of numbers, or a series of snapshots, taken over a series of days.

Yet, every single day, those of us in schools send messages of hope and reward, messages of the efficacy of individual initiative, and we tell the stories of those who have overcome. We teach that individuals can make change happen, and then we watch regretfully as those whom we have taught become disillusioned, further disenfranchised, disempowered, and finally despondent because the world outside of schools resists change with the weight of generations and the power of prestige and politics.

We send learners from schools holding the future of our nation in their hands, armed with what we offered. Some of our students are given a legacy of success, of academic stardom from schools that were complete with up-to-the-minute technology and outstanding instructors. Those are the students who were often most able to pay the fees to compete in the best sports, practice in the best facilities, take lessons outside of school, and travel during breaks. Yet others are sent forth from our schools armed with legacies of failure, of not living up to expectations, from places where they were invisible, and where they were given messages of being undeserving from the first day of school forward.

All of our students learn that their votes will count, that in this country everyone has an equal chance, and that every citizen in this nation is given a voice and the freedom to use it. Our students in our schools believe that this nation was founded on principles of equality, and that this country cares about the lives of children from every walk of life.

I have grown up, over the course of a long career in education, to believe that those of us who are out of school owe those who are in schools consideration of the ideals we would have them learn. If we teach them to believe in the American Dream, then we must work to make that dream possible, or we must admit to supporting a lie.

We have to acknowledge that what happens in Saint Paul, and in Washington, D.C., affects the lives of our children in classrooms, immediately and immensely, and we cannot vote for platforms that destroy dreams for children. The mission and vision for our public schools is composed and maintained by those whom we elect. We owe our children the honor of a promise that holds truth. We need to weigh carefully candidates' stands on issues of children and schools. We need to pay attention, and vote accordingly, or shoulder a shame that will become our own sad and defining legacy, if not our undoing altogether.

Throwing Darts and Money

We have to find a way to make sure that schools and those who support schools can communicate about what matters to each, to share expectations and to find meaningful ways of solving problems.

IT SEEMS THAT EVERYWHERE I TURN, every time I pick up a publication or listen to discussion on the radio or television, I am once again subjected to someone's rantings about "No Child Left Behind." The federal Act, which governs the distribution of federal entitlement funds to America's schools, has been relabeled "No Child Left Untested," "No School Left Unscathed," "No Teacher Left Alone," and "No Way, No How" in the vernacular. No Child Left Behind came on the scene a couple of years ago when Congress renewed the Elementary and Secondary Education Act, which originated in part as a response to Sputnik and was a vehicle to provide extra help to kids at risk.

For those who decry the fact that the Act is too wordy, I feel I need to remind them that it is legislation.

For those who attempt to break down the funding formulas and explain the disbursements and monitoring through state agencies, I have to say, "Good luck." I think it was a recent former Minnesota governor and wrestler who claimed that funding for public schools is so complicated that only two people in the whole state really understand it. I think that was an optimistic statement. Now, with the addition of federal regulations and new compliance requirements—well, that pool of understanders narrows even further.

The fact is that we get money from the feds to help us provide programs, assistance, and consideration for students who do not come to school from a level playing field. Federal monies received under the No Child Left Behind Act (NCLB) are used to assist children whose first language is not English, or who come from homes where economic circumstances are not conducive to study or ambient reading. NCLB funds are used to enroll and provide for students from migrant families and homeless families. These funds help to assist us so that within schools we provide more equal opportunities regardless of gender, ethnicity, or income. The list goes on and on.

NCLB monies are not earmarked to pay for all special education services. Students identified under a separate set of criteria use a separate funding formula. NCLB monies are not used to build new buildings. The money that runs our schools and pays most teachers and turns on the heat in the winter comes from state and district sources, not from NCLB.

The funding that we get from the feds to try to make things more equal, however, is substantial—somewhere in the neighborhood of 120 million dollars annually in Minnesota. So, regardless of the fact that the allocation does not turn the lights on, it would make a big dent in what we do if it disappeared. It would also make dubious sense

The spirit of the law and the intent of the lawmakers or the law abiders simply cannot be to destroy the institution.

to taxpayers if this money were given to states to give to schools without any way of seeing what happens when we spend it. I imagine that Defense, Transportation, and other departments are subject to accountability for spending. I cannot imagine any legislator going back to a constituency and saying, "Well, we just gave them the money, and someone must have used it somehow."

Of course, nothing is simple in education. In other state and federal departments, one can count and measure and determine the return on investment, pretty much. In education, the idea of "return on investment" supposes that we could control the variables at some point. We can't. We are not making widgets. We have no access to the gene pool. We are not in charge of who moves where and why, and what jobs are lost and found, and what happens to a child in the hours other than the seven or so, spent five days a week, for several months a year, in school. Measurement of success in schools, therefore, gets so darn messy and mushy.

So, in the midst of this mess and mushiness, the mud starts to fly. Schools feel afraid of the sanctions suffered as consequences for not being able to do impossible tasks. Legislators cannot know the complexities of everyday life among schoolchildren, and yet are expected by voters to provide results. Each is asking the impossible from the other.

The spirit of the law and the intent of the lawmakers or the law abiders simply cannot be to destroy the institution. At least, I really hope that is not the case. NCLB asks each state to determine a set of standards in math, reading, language arts, and science that will be used to measure all students. It also asks schools to gather data from the measurements created, and break up that data. It asks that we analyze the information and look at the scores from the groups of students served by the funding provided. In other words, we are to look at the scores of those students who are migrant, for whom English is a second language, those identified as needing special services, ethnic minorities enrolled, and those students who receive free or reduced-cost school lunches. If any of those groups in schools that receive federal funding are found to score low on the tests created to measure the standards, then the school is asked to concentrate efforts on those children or face a set of consequences.

The consequences become cumbersome after two years or more of forced concentration. Schools will be asked to provide tutoring and transfer. Eventually, without showing adequate improvement, schools will be reconstituted. No school in Minnesota is there yet.

There are so many who sit on either side of this fence and cluck their tongues and shake their heads and point their fingers. To smugly second-guess an educator or a legislator seems to be the bailiwick of darn near everyone.

Inevitably, if something is too cumbersome, it implodes. We all have seen it happen time and time again. Inevitably, if enough people complain about a particular piece of legislation, it becomes modified or thrown away in a political bid to appease a block of voters. We are already seeing modification to the interpretation of NCLB. Inevitably, there will be more legislation to follow. Inevitably, we will balk under new misinformed restrictions, expectations, and punishments.

Given time and distance, the dance between the lawmakers and the educators seems a little sad. Indeed, what is asked of public schools is too much. And yet, by tuning into the intent of legislation, it may be possible to hear the voice of the people we depend on for our existence. There is a possibility that, through NCLB, the taxpayers are asking that we look more closely this go-round at the groups that tend to get lost in the average scores. Maybe we are being asked to pay even closer attention to those who are falling out, and falling in between, the cracks. Maybe we do not have accurate measurements of student achievement that could provide this information. Maybe we need to get some.

In spite of the threats, the bombast, the incredulity, and the cries for emancipation that emanate from the public and published opinions on this issue, I cannot help but believe that in schools, where the real work happens, teachers and administrators are looking at what can be done and doing it. I also cannot help but believe that those elected to serve us, when it really comes down to the face in the mirror, cast their votes believing that they are doing what is right by all of us. I cannot believe otherwise. There are those who claim that despite our best efforts, there is a plot to destroy public schools. Why would anyone who is pledged to uphold and defend our constitution want to do that?

There have to be places where we—taxpayers, lawmakers, and educators—trust each others' motives. I would hope that one such place would be among innocent children in our public schools. As most schoolchildren could tell you, the reason we raise our hands in school is so that we all can listen and be heard. It's a lesson in respect and trust taught early and often, and yet it is easy to forget when the stakes begin to rise beyond reason and we start to think that we possess the only voice in the room that matters.

Tulips, Two Years, and
Too Many Promises

···

Each legislative session seems to see issues of education funding
come to the forefront. Every two years, schools in Minnesota are allocated
funds, based on what's important to whom at that time. For decades,
funding for students in classrooms has simply not kept up with inflation
and expectations of schools to provide extensive services.

IT IS RAINY, BUT WARM—just right for encouraging tulips and daffodils, and creating crabgrass. We have had beautiful days and warm nights, and there just could not be a better place to live than here, right now, but I am weary and disheartened. I am tired of those who consistently seem to think that there are easy answers to complex questions. And I am tired of getting my hopes up for support in the form of funding for schools.

Every two years, the state legislature votes to appropriate funding for public schools. Every two years, the Omnibus K-12 Finance Bill is up for rewrite and re-vote and changes and debate. Every two years, we seem to enter the session hopeful. We get hopeful based on promises. Promises always include rhetoric praising the work of teachers, praising the work of schools, extolling the importance of reaching children, of providing for the future, of not letting us down, of pledging to be the "Education Governor, Mayor, President, Senator, whatever." But, for the past two decades, schools have seen cuts and cuts and more cuts. Now, we are afraid of more years of cuts. There is nothing left to cut. The buildings are bleeding.

It seems so easy for critics to point to school practices and blame public servants for failing to fix a multitude of societal problems. Some seem to believe that if we identify a small portion of the expectations of schools and measure those expectations often and with vigor, schools will shape up. Others seem to think that we are simply getting more money, but the complicated answer is that we are not. I have often thought that anyone who has gone to school seems to have an opinion on running schools. Because of that, we find the expectations growing, the demand for better opportunities growing, the demand for more highly skilled graduates growing, the demand for better services for all our children growing, but the actual means by which to live up to those expectations is shrinking. We can't do it all.

None of us can do it all. I just sat through two hours of listening to a group of student teachers. These bright and eager men and women are currently finishing their degrees and are completing their internships in schools. Their stories should be mandatory listening for legislators, I think. Our student teachers wondered if they should take the initiative to call parents in order to discuss problem students if they know that the call means that the child may be harmed. They wondered how to best support their pregnant teens in classrooms, grieving students in classrooms, children who can't do homework because they live in cars, children whose parents are gravely ill, in jail, or simply not home most of the time. Our student teachers wanted advice on handling the pressure to pass students, raise test scores, and teach with no texts, no paper, no guidance, and no faith from the community. Our students told us of the kids who waited by their classrooms in the morning, kids who didn't want to stay home because there was no heat, no food, or no peace. They spoke of kids who are afraid to go home, every day.

I believe that anyone who wants schools to cut back, to retool, or to stop "riding the gravy train" needs to spend ten months, from dawn till dusk, in public schools, among schoolchildren, receiving the blessings of being among them and some enlightenment as to the real world of schools today. I think then that simple solutions would be exposed for the hypocrisy that they are.

I have heard talk that some districts have considered fewer school days. Others think about shutting down for the month of January, and others are cutting sports and cheerleading and debate and transportation—program after program, opportunity after opportunity, and lifeline after lifeline. Insurance rates soar; salaries raise a little bit; the cost of services leaps up; and the funding stays flat. We have no fat to cut. Some schools will have to start cutting the bones.

This week and next week, our legislators will be deciding the funding for public schools. What started this session as higher hopes than we have had in some time has progressed to few hopes as the bills start to appear. We still can call. We still can be heard, I think. At some point we really do need to invest in our future, in our children. What else could there be that is of more value, of more potential, or of more importance?

Nice Catch

· ·

Risking real change in schools is a rare and often individual act of teachers.
Large change in public schools is even more rare.

I THINK I HAVE LIVED WITH, IN, AND AROUND Catch-22 situations for
most of my very long career, come to think of it! In the field of education,
we are encouraged to change, to try new things, to make schools better;
yet our funding is tied to increased test scores and increased compliance
with the status quo. Researchers Caine and Caine, who have explored
the topic of brain-based teaching (1997), conclude that most schools
use traditional methods of teaching and that school boards and district
level management endorse just
that. Our beliefs as societies
are based on how schools were
organized during the Industrial
Age, and most of our beliefs
and experiences do not reflect
current and advanced research
in teaching and learning. Because of our widely differing orientations,
most changes to schools and school systems are only surface level.

We tried to change teaching
and learning
at the instructional core...

Several years ago in Minnesota, the state spent hundreds of thousands
of dollars and hundreds of thousands of hours trying to implement some
of the complex changes that research has found necessary to change education for the future. We tried to organize knowledge and understanding into
cross-curricular categories and to require performance assessment instead
of traditional measurements. We tried to change teaching and learning at
the instructional core, but the means by which this shift was implemented,
the huge need for so much new learning on the part of resistant faculties,
and the unfamiliarity of the public regarding schools that didn't do things

"regular" was just too much. In some instances, the changes were top-down and top-heavy and unclear. In other situations, the requirements were at first resisted and then embraced. In the end, the project was scrapped, and more traditional standards and testing methods were adopted instead. I was part of the grand experiment, and I saw the spark when things happened that were very right for kids. I know that many teachers and many schools kept the good and will always keep the good, but that strong pull to the status quo is, I think, our biggest problem.

In my experience, the ones who resist change have learned to do so because "this year's new things" always come and go. They have learned to just wait it out until the annoyances go away. And they have always been proven right. We are such a huge institution, and we attract those who have been successful with the status quo, and therefore, ours is a very hard institution to change. It is no wonder that innovators are usually operating in downshift mode! When one lives in fear of losing face, work, or funding, one cannot help but downshift.

However, a core of like minds exists in any faculty, no matter where, that cannot stand still, who want to make things better no matter what, and who are willing to try new things. Depending on their success with various initiatives, more and more faculty become willing to try based on the efforts of this brave faction. There are, and probably always will be, those teachers who are willing to engage while downshifting, risk while downshifting, and work against the Catch-22. I think we are moved to join that group of experimenters when what we have learned about new best practice captures our emotion and our conscience, and we can't not take the risk set before us.

Deciding Who Wins from a Distance

··

Educators, parents, and citizens are being asked to decide where to put the priorities in allocating funds and determining programs. Not enough funding has been allocated for schools to do well at both ends of the spectrum of needs.

I WOULD HOPE THAT IT WILL be very hard to decide which children will be the ones left behind in the end, after all the politicking and the hoopla.

I just finished talking with probably one of the best mothers, ever. She has young children in public schools, right here in our area, and she is really worried about her son. He is a very bright boy. He was placed in a class, a hands-on class, with thirty-some classmates. Half of his classmates were classified as being "at risk." Another 25 percent were special needs students. Her boy would come home angry each day, at not being able to hear the teacher or to concentrate. So, the mom, being a really great mom, called the teacher.

The teacher had no answers, only sadness, so this mom called the principal. She asked what she could do to help. The principal had no answers, either, at all.

She is wondering whether it's time to move her son to a private school, or to a charter, or to a school in a nearby town. She doesn't want him not to be challenged. She doesn't want him to be taught less well than other children, in other schools.

What a place we find ourselves in these days! We have politicians who tell us that we need to line kids up to go right from middle school to engineering, from ninth grade health to brain surgery, and they are right. We do need to provide our country and our world with engineers and scientists, or we will lose an edge, miss opportunities.

We are also faced with classrooms filled with students who, for myriad reasons, cannot learn at the pace of those ready to fly away to universities. These are the kids who need incredible attention, who cannot concentrate, who need to establish their identities by being rebellious, becoming outlaws. These are the kids who need to be taught in new and sensitive ways, who require extra time, extra care.

There are politicians and reformers who say that those kids, the ones who need extra help, are part of the accountability for schools. The ones least responsive to traditional teaching are the ones who show up on our great big tests as "underperforming." Those kids are the ones who dunk schools into "Needs Improvement" status and bring sanctions upon sites under the No Child Left Behind legislation.

The politicians are right again. We do need to pay attention, to be accountable for those kids, too.

So, there you have it. We need to create and maintain a pool of extraordinary technical and scientific innovators, students who are ready and able to lead the world to a better place, at least technologically. We also need to make sure that each child in school has a plan for post-secondary school. And we need to figure out ways to reach students with real and difficult obstacles to learning or face the loss of even more dollars.

So, someone will have to decide at some point. Where will the funding go?

We have a very large order to fill. And we don't, as of yet anyway, have the resources to do any of those items very well.

Perhaps during this session, our state and federal legislators will provide for schools an unprecedented increase in funding, clearly earmarked for specific results, in numbers and categories sufficient to address the needs of our most needy and to provide opportunities for students with promise (all students).

Perhaps, but unlikely.

So, someone will have to decide at some point. Where will the funding go? Will it go toward the kids on the edge of genius, those with recognized potential to save us all and invent the next really great thing? Or will we focus our funds on making sure that all students have the skills to survive?

Survive or thrive? Is it OK for us to focus on bringing students to universities at the expense of sentencing some to hopelessness? Is it OK to focus funding on those with the most needs at the expense of those who could soar above us all?

We can try, but we cannot do both very well. We are leaky at the seams, and our buckets are full to bursting.

I just hope that whoever does the deciding, whoever makes the decision regarding which end to feed and which end to starve, spends many sleepless nights tossing and turning and agonizing over this choice. I hope whoever makes the decision has to go home to families with children at both ends of the spectrum. If someone makes a choice to deny a future to some children, that person needs to live with the children denied.

Schools cannot go on much longer under the delusion that they can do all that they are asked to do without more help. We are going to need that decider, pretty soon.

We'd probably better start thinking about whom we can trust with such a choice.

Opryland and Opportunity, Oh My!

What happened in Nashville was a chance to see how things could be done differently, presented by folks who had done things differently.

BEING HOME, IN DULUTH, surrounded by the heavy heat of a summer night is a far cry from the artificial environment that literally encloses acres and acres inside a hotel and convention center in Nashville, Tennessee. I prefer Duluth, mosquitoes and all, but what happened in Nashville just can't stay in Nashville.

What happened in Nashville was the Thirteenth Annual Model Schools Conference—five solid days of sessions, keynotes, and featured speakers presenting their innovations, theories, and successes, sharing resources and stories of effective leadership and transformed schools to thousands of educators from across the country. Our little delegation from Duluth became elated, afraid, enlightened, and inspired, depending on the sessions attended. We met at the beginning and at the end of every day to plan how the few of us could cover the most ground and to debrief and share what we had discovered. We did not break for lunches or breakfasts; instead, we attended sessions from the opening bell to the closing bell each day.

We heard from schools that sprouted in the middle of inner cities that promised each student a paid-for college education upon graduation, and they delivered. We heard from high schools where every teacher became a teacher of math, of reading, and of writing. We listened to teachers and counselors and principals who led schools to remove all remedial classes, who provided two years of math delivered in one year, and who created different, individual plans and projects for each student in attendance. We heard from schools that ran three separate and distinct schedules in one building, districts that used blocks, four-hour classes, nine weeks on and two weeks off, year-round schools, who had half the staff come in early and half stay late in the day, and some that made the senior year the most rigorous of all.

We heard about schools in Florida, Texas, Colorado, Oregon, Virginia, Rhode Island, Tennessee, California, and places in between. We listened to stories about schools with mournful funding situations and tales about those with seemingly unlimited funds. We heard from dreamers and visionaries, and those who do the hard work of making dreams into realities in institutions with limited space, support, and faith from the community.

We heard from leaders who said, "Be bold!" We heard others who said, "Go slow, and get everyone on board!" Some just said, "Communicate!" There were futurists who talked about how our economy is different, communication is different, students are different, and learning is different. We saw data that illustrated how our technology is making so much of what we do now obsolete, how globalization and our changing demographics will require a moral response from schools, and how our changing attitudes toward work are leaving our students ill-prepared for a very competitive world.

We literally sat in the Grand Ol' Opry and watched star-struck presenting researchers from the Gates Foundation walk to center stage, stand on the star, and yell "Howdy!" to the crowd before projecting spreadsheets on the big screen and digging in to the statistics at hand that showed the trends in successful schools. We were told to aim toward smaller learning communities, personalization, individualization, rigor, and relevance, and to establish priorities because we can't be all things to all people and do anything well. We need focus, sharp and true, and energy, and passion, and the only thing that should scare us to death is the inability to face ourselves honestly.

We found, in Nashville, reasons to celebrate and reasons to gnash our teeth. We recall the words of keynote speaker Dr. Willard R. Daggert, who said, "We have to educate our children for their future, not our past." What happened in Nashville was a wake-up call and a siren song, set to the strains of a fiddle and a steel guitar. One thing we know for sure is that each of those successful presenting schools believed in what they were doing. They found common beliefs and common purpose, and they stuck with their beliefs and acted on them.

This ain't no practice life. These ain't no practice kids. Their futures will not include everyone riding off into the sunset, tall in the saddles, unless we, too, turn around and face the sunrise and decide what it is we believe in strongly enough to act together to achieve.

We do need to think about it seriously, y'all.

Mods and Pods and Hanging Out

....

It has been said that you can tell the values of a district by the schedule chosen at the high school. At a glance, one can see whether music, art, physical fitness, time on a subject sufficient for labs or discussions, and room for electives have been provided.

WHEN I DID MY STUDENT TEACHING, somewhere back in the last century, we were in "mods." I don't mean we dressed "mod." I was born just a teeny bit too late for that wave of incredible chicness. I am of the generation of poly-knit double-ester. I wore some knit something when I was a student teacher, but I worked in "mods." We marked time, divided our days, and taught our students using the "new best thing" of those years—modular scheduling.

I was a student teacher at Hopkins Lindbergh High School. An airplane hung from the ceiling in the middle of the building. The halls were all carpeted so students could sit down on the floors, whenever, and departments were housed in wings built around pods and centers. We teachers each had desks in the department office, and no one had a permanent classroom. We met with students as scheduled in various locations in our wings. We were so very modern. We were so very chic. And, we just knew so darn much.

I know less now.

My fading memory faintly signals that a "mod" was a twenty-minute block of time. I think I taught my Roots in American Literature course for two mods every day except Fridays. I taught my Writing to Find Yourself (or something) course for three mods, a couple of days a week. The flexibility of the system was enormous.

Each student had individual schedules, with separate arrival and departure times, and there were always students sitting in the halls, in the commons, in the pods, because there were always students with unscheduled time. It's true that a few students used their time to do research in the library, but most seemed to just hang out. They seemed stalwart in their lack of productivity. It was also pretty difficult for adults in the building to differentiate the students hanging out from young, random drug dealers and other itinerant visitors, since everyone seemed to come and go at will, and they all dressed alike.

In my opinion, neither student teachers nor students are ever really ready to maximize class periods or manage time well when faced with increased opportunities to hang out.

Students are still attracted to hanging out, I think. That capacity will need to be considered as school boards determine what schedules at high schools will look like next year and the years after that.

We really do need to choose schedules that aren't just "this year's new thing." In the same vein, I do hope we don't choose schedules based only on what we have done before, either. Schedule choosing should reflect an understanding of new best practices, the need for flexibility, and the need for increased rigor and relevance for our students. The schedule does need to be legal, of course, fiscally responsible, obviously, and it must have the support of the unions. It must allow for betterment, for considered risk taking, and for increased opportunities for all students. I also hope it provides pathways for collaboration and cooperation between buildings, and that it helps to redistribute students to reduce the enormous class sizes that are choking systems. A new schedule needs to allow for growth in our understanding of what it will take to thrive in the next decades and beyond.

We cannot do what we always have done, because the world has changed, and opportunities may pass us by. We cannot choose based on past practice, because past practice is being informed by new understandings. We cannot settle for change that is easy simply because it is easy. We may need to look to change some of our own assumptions and points of view in order to see our way clear to providing something better for our kids.

There are hundreds of possible scheduling options out there for high schools. From block schedules to alternate day, to part-block, and all-day, every-day school from seven until seven. Then there are hybrids and modifications, and there are schools that support each and every one—

schools that have found huge success for students using any of the above championed models. A change of schedule should bring excitement and energy, concentration and consideration enough to bring fresh air into tired institutions. A new schedule should bring new dreams and new visions and inspiring possibilities.

Personally, I can't support the bringing back of modular schedules. Been there. Done that. There were some serious flaws. However, the idea that we can change and take a risk and design something that holds the promise of more and better options is what keeps a lot of us alive, wakes us up in the morning, and sends us joyfully to the closet to find some polyester to put on and go on in to work.

Trouble, Trends, and Taking Action

···

We have a choice when presented with criticism.
We can take it, or see where it leaves us.

THERE'S TROUBLE OUT THERE. I was recently handed an executive summary of the Citizens League Report on Higher Education in Minnesota (November 2004), and I see trouble. The League tells us that, "As an inland state with a reputation for up to six months of winter, education is Minnesota's most important economic and quality-of-life resource. But global economic and local demographic challenges threaten our competitive advantage in higher education."

The report goes on to tell us a lot of things, such as:

- We currently rank eighth in the country as a high-tech state, but we can't get junior and senior high students to take higher-level math and science.
- Minnesota is in the bottom half of the states in terms of science and engineering degrees as a percentage of total degrees granted.
- Over 30 percent of graduates from Minnesota high schools need remediation classes in order to begin higher education.
- Other countries are surpassing the United States in higher education participation. The United States ranking has slipped from second to fifteenth in just twelve years.

I hate information like this! I am not sure where the Citizens League found this information, but it's out there. And it makes me uncomfortable. It makes me feel like we should *respond* somehow and *do* something. I wish I could just dismiss this stuff, and disregard it, but I am very aware of the fact that only one of our own six children is pursuing an engineering degree. And he is working his tail off to get it. We haven't done our part.

The Citizens League does make some recommendations. Most of its recommendations are beyond our circle of influence, but a couple of them caught my eye and my imagination and gave me a hunk of hope. The first one was the recommendation that we increase expectations—in high school and in higher education. This recommendation could be pretty timely for us, you know. In Duluth, especially, as we plan for the future of our schools, this recommendation is one that should be heeded. The League suggests some reform strategies to achieve the increased expectations, including that we:

- Raise expectations to at least two years of post–high school education as a minimum level of academic achievement for every Minnesotan. In a knowledge economy, a high school diploma is not sufficient.

- Make better use of time spent in high school, and ensure that all students are ready for higher education. This includes a required higher education preparatory curriculum for all students, improved access to higher education opportunities (e.g., advanced placement and post-secondary education options for students who are ready, and great remediation and access for students who are not yet prepared for higher education).

- Invest: Minnesota should increase its investment in improving the co-ordination and expansion of college readiness and access programs.

Dang! I love these ideas! What if we stopped thinking K-12 and started thinking K-14? What if we tied our colleges and our technical schools to high school campuses in our cities? Instead of thinking of school as "a place to go," we could start thinking about school as "a state of learning—a state of being taught." We could see school as a continuing process, with smooth transitions from high school to higher learning, with permeable borders for a virtual community of learners!

The thing is, we don't have to think of school as we have always thought of school. We know that so many jobs that folks do now just plain didn't exist five, or even two, years ago. We know that our high school students will probably work in situations we have not even conceived of yet. We also know that if a robot can do it, a robot will do it, so we cannot afford to send our beloved children out into a world where they have few skills to survive, let alone thrive. None of our kids deserve that!

The Citizens League recommends that we "establish pilot K-14 programs with select community/technical colleges and local K-12 districts." I'd like to add colleges and universities to that mix as well, and go for it.

I'd just love to see schools break out of old molds and become radiant with possibilities! Just think, "Duluth 9-14 Institutes!" Wouldn't that just be something for everyone to brag about?

Darn Paper, Darn Topic, Darn Potholes Everywhere

Education finance is so complex that most of us don't want to think about it.
The dispersal of funds, however, illuminates our values and our priorities.

I AM WRITING A DARN PAPER. I would like to use language that better expresses how I feel about this darn paper-writing experience, especially regarding the darn topic I was forced to consider, but I just can't do it out loud. Darn it! I am writing about education finance. Now, do you understand my frustration?

The thing is, just when one thinks one has a handle on financing schools in our state, the spreadsheet wraps around itself and comes alive. It's true. The exceptions are just plain exceptional. We have allocation formulas that are like monsters in dark closets. We have buried inequities and rules that contradict one another, and it all winds up somehow paying for salaries and equipment and facilities, in much the same way it has for thirty years, but I really don't know anyone who can fully explain every piece of it…or would want to. And I can't imagine anyone who would want to listen to a full explanation, anyway.

But, here's the thing. We have to pay attention. We do. Because the truth is that we can talk social change, accountability, equality, creating a great society, a just world, and an informed electorate, etc., all we want, but we know it's all just words and platitudes unless action happens. And action just doesn't happen on a scale as large as public schools unless there is funding attached. OK, without funding wonderful things still do happen, but funding provides a pretty hefty lever, so we just have to follow the winding funding streams to see what is provided for, to find what is supposed to happen on a large scale.

If we follow the money, we can see what it is the taxpayers are willing to support, and we need to pay attention to that. We need to pay attention to that because if we work for a public institution we are not self-employed. We need to listen to our bosses. When we forget to listen, well, we risk lack of support or losing the stream altogether.

By accepting the money, those of us who do work for public institutions enter into a contract of sorts. The public tells us, through legislation and allocation, what it wants us to do, and if we accept the funding, we agree to try to do what is mandated. It becomes an ethical issue at that point. If the taxpayers tell the public schools that they are requiring some form of accountability, whether we agree or not, if we take the money, we accept the job as described. We do have the right to moan, spit, complain, criticize, protest, and suggest alternatives, but we do not have the right not to comply. If the taxpayers provide funding aimed at a particular population (social targeting) or toward the implementation of a particular program (could be anything), we need to comply. We can't accept the money and aim for a different target. We are not self-employed. We are public servants.

It is because of the ethics part and the targeting part mandated by federal, state, and local governments that the funding gets so darned confusing. Public policy analysts synthesize the issues down into just two words: *equity* and *adequacy*. As taxpayers, do we try to fund schools in such a way that every child receives the same amount of money? Or do we try to fund schools at a level that guarantees that every student learns at least a specified amount of learning? Do we aim toward equity or adequacy?

Our state is unique in that our constitution calls for the creation of a general, uniform, thorough, and efficient system of public schools. Our founders believed that the success of a republic rests in the knowledge of its citizens. The only other constitutional allocation in our state is the one to provide for a system of highways. Still, there are potholes all over. More in some places.

Ethics and money are not always tied together, yet in working through the issues of funding public schools, the philosophies of those with the purse strings eventually show up in dollars for districts. When the dollars enter the accounts of our districts, the dispersing and the prioritizing rest in the hands of our superintendents and our school board members. We, as taxpayers, allocate the money every time we vote. It's important that whenever we choose new superintendents or other leaders, we do ask the questions about finance that reveal the thinking in the offices at which the buck stops. Will a new leader aim for equity (seeing all as deserving of the same) or adequacy (holding the funding accountable for a level of learning for all even when that means that some will receive more and others less)?

Someone just needs to ask the darn questions. Someone else just needs to write her darn paper.

Rummage Sales and Rumblings

....

Sometimes, it is a paraprofessional who makes a teacher's work possible.
Often, it is a paraprofessional who sees what we don't see and makes the
connection with a child that makes all the difference.

SUDDENLY, THEY WERE EVERYWHERE.

Little, beautiful Hutchinson, Minnesota, lies perfectly pastoral one day, and then—whoosh. They descend. They drive in from Litchfield, Esko, Willmar, Fergus Falls, points East, North, South, and whatever sits West, and of course, some come from The Cities. They leave no room at the inns. They are tall, tiny, wispy, mighty, and everything in between. They look like dimpled grammas and young fashion models and gramma fashion models, too.

They laugh easily and heartily. They eat well. And they welcome one another and everyone else to Ridgewater College for their weekend. Hutchinsonites host hundreds of garage sales during this weekend. Vendors at the college sell educational programs, jewelry, appliquéd clothing, and pretty crafts. The union is there. And there are door prizes, a big table of them, wrapped in fancy bags with tissues and ribbons and frothiness.

Last weekend was the Minnesota Paraprofessionals Conference in Hutchinson, where that same conference has been held for the past eleven years. The paraprofessionals in attendance were overwhelmingly, but not exclusively, female, and as I looked out over the hundreds of folk in the audience, I saw the apple-cheeked faces of tangible progress in public education. I did. Here they were, on a Friday night and then all day Saturday, on a beautiful weekend in the spring, inside this school, learning for the sake of it. Here they were, attending sessions on one-on-one tutoring, behavior management, keeping attention, keeping records, safety, and of course, learning how to become or remain in compliance with No Child Left Behind.

Several of those who had been around this conference for the past several years told me that there was energy at this one that had fear attached to it. They told me to look into the eyes of the people at the sessions and see the sadness, the anger, and the darting vision of the afraid. They told me that the para's are afraid of the law, afraid of compliance, and afraid that the jobs they hold so dear could be jerked out of their reach. The para's are waiting for their districts to tell them what they will need to do to keep working. Some districts have decided. Many have not. Paraprofessionals are waiting to hear if they have to go back to school, take instruction, take a test, or take a hike.

They are waiting in silence in most places. Although there are some thirty thousand paraprofessionals in Minnesota, they are not a cacophony. They hold jobs that, until now, required no formal training in most cases. They take their places every day beside teachers in classrooms, on playgrounds, in lunchrooms, in media centers, on buses, and in hallways and doorways, and they help. They help with homework. They help to translate. They work the wheelchairs, the machines, and the paper, and they tie shoes, carry books, find mittens, and hold hands. They prevent fights and frustration. They clean up. They anticipate.

They were not there when I was in school. I remember a girl in a wheelchair whose mother came to school many times a day to carry her and the chair up and down the granite staircase in order that she could attend classes just like the rest of us. I remember the mother lovingly lifting her daughter out of the chair and into the bathroom at noon because the chair didn't fit. There were no para's then. I don't remember the girl and her mom much past junior high. I don't know if they both just got tired, or ill, but she was gone. We just stopped seeing her around. We stopped seeing a lot of kids. After about sixth grade, we stopped seeing the children of the migrant poultry workers. They quit coming to school. After about the tenth grade, the real troublemakers, the very bad boys and the obnoxious girls, disappeared and were not seen in school again. The ones who never really learned to read dropped out as soon as they could. There was a wing attached to the building where there must have been special education classes, but we didn't see those kids either, really. Some of our classmates quit coming in order to work the farms. Some kids seemed to be sick a lot and never really did come, ever, so we never really looked for them, either.

We went to a school that looked like us. But there were presidents and lawmakers during those times who saw schools as places where democracy and the belief that we are equal, that all children deserve the dream, needed to become reality. Those giant thinkers funded programs and purposes in our schools that specifically reached out to children of migrant families, children who had no homes, children living in poverty, those whose first language was not English, and children whose situations carried the risk of unequal access to opportunity. Those in power at that time also envisioned potential for children who were diagnosed with disabilities that caused learning and behavior barriers. It is because of legislation enacted at that time that we have paraprofessionals in our schools.

The children my generation stopped seeing, or never did see, are the children the para's serve. Every day, paraprofessionals see the children we would not. And every day, those children see themselves through the eyes of schools that want them there. Those children see themselves as important, and worthy of special attention, extra help, and a smile and a wink and a welcome.

And now, the entitlements created back then to level the playing field have been reauthorized under the umbrella called No Child Left Behind. The reauthorization requires that all paraprofessionals serving the children identified under the titled programs become "highly qualified." Districts must hire folk with special training. Those para's who currently hold jobs will now need to pass tests or take courses, or both, depending on their district's decision.

Many wait anxiously for those decisions. In the meantime, they smile, bring brownies, keep pencils in their pockets, and they see and reach children. They see and reach the children who need them, and whom they have learned to hold dear. Once a year, hundreds and hundreds of them drive to Hutchinson. They give up a weekend in order to see and reach out to one another.

They come to Hutchinson each year as the tulips burst forth to become vibrant. You cannot help but see the overwhelming beauty of such important flowers in such large and organized brilliant masses. No one beholding such a gathering could miss seeing them as the precious and powerful gifts that they are, and that they were meant to be.

Numbers and Fear

....

Generation of numbers is not the problem. We can generate a lot of
numbers by mandated tests of students in classrooms.
The question is whether we are producing numbers that mean anything at all.

IT SEEMS WE ARE LIVING IN A WORLD OF DATA. Numbers, and correlates of numbers, test scores, survey responses, feasibility coefficients, and their interrelatedness with one another seem to provide bases for a whole lot of decisions made by schools. We slice and cobble together numbers and scores, grades, expenditures, and attendance records, and we send in sheaves of compiled data to all kinds of agencies that compile more.

I spent this day pouring over data myself. I actually really like doing just that (it's a sickness, I know). I love looking past perception to see if a hypothesis can stand in the face of evidence from multiple indicators. However, I did find myself thinking hard today about whether we are getting the evidence we need, or whether we are just getting a lot of evidence.

We can't measure confidence, initiative, kindness, or whether a learner knows his or her own strengths by using fill-in-the-blank tests.

In this era of No Child Left Behind, we have generated numbers like never before, especially test scores. Valid test scores (if they are a measure of what we believe to be important) could help schools make plans to close teaching gaps. Such scores, however, are awfully hard to get on a large scale.

We can't measure confidence, initiative, kindness, or whether or not a learner knows his or her own strengths by using fill-in-the-blank tests. We can't measure whether a learner could perform a task or solve a new problem in a real world situation with a Number 2 pencil, nor can we determine whether that learner can lead, follow, or contribute. We don't find our poets, economists, inventors, thinkers, or visual artists through the tests delivered en masse, under controlled conditions.

We can't see growth using these tests, either. They do not indicate whether a school made giant leaps of progress. We can't tell by looking at the state test scores whether the students came in the door already reading, whether they learned to read, or whether they first learned to speak English and then learned to read English before taking the tests. We can't tell if a student's score reflects the fact that he or she spent the year before fleeing across a desert, witnessing unspeakable acts of violence, and losing everything and everyone before taking the tests. We can't even tell whether a score reflects a morning at home with Cheerios, fruit, and a kiss, or a dark, cold, and hungry start to the day.

I love data, and I am afraid of data. I love it that we can look and question why. I love it that we are asked to examine our practices in light of actual numbers. But I am afraid of losing some wonderful purpose and passionate vision in the process if we are not sensitive and aware of who is getting punished by the same law that requires the data.

Data is neutral. It has no meaning until meaning is assigned. A number is a number, a comparison a comparison, until we decide how we want to frame those comparisons. I am coming to believe that amateurs and politicians can't make those meanings for schools, because the meanings cannot be simple. The contexts and the situations that produce those scores are incredibly complex.

Good schools and good test scores are not necessarily carried in the same bucket. Schools that provide a place and a way of teaching and learning that enable giant growth for students who have not been served well elsewhere are good schools, but they cannot deliver the same scores as schools that do not undertake the challenge of serving those children. Schools that are located in geographical areas where immigrants have always first settled will most likely always have enrollees with no English. Those schools will provide giant leaps of growth, but the scores will not be as high as in places where everyone comes in the door speaking the language of the classrooms. Schools designed to provide different ways of learning for students who have been disenfranchised (or who have left the traditional system in despair and disillusionment) have been shown to turn lives around, but the scores will still reflect the years of difficulty. Schools located in areas where economics require that everyone works, or in places where tradition and culture have labeled public schools as places of punishment and discrimination, can make magnificent gains, but the playing field is simply not even.

It's summer, dang it. It's time to revel in the magnificence of our lake, the sunshine, and our green trees. But it is also a time when schools begin to make decisions for next year. Now is the season of looking at the numbers. I hope we do. But I also hope we think hard about who gets punished, again, when we place meaning and blame using neutral data. Decisions about schools should never be just about the facts. They should always and only be just about the children.

Fire, Wines, and the Sounds of Music

· ·

Music and the arts are often set aside in schools these days,
due to the emphasis on writing, reading, and math
required by state testing and federal legislation.

ONE TIME, JUST ABOUT SIX YEARS AGO, a group of my friends and I
burned down our sauna. We didn't mean to, of course. We were a "Birthday
Group," and we got together monthly or so and celebrated and talked and
laughed. It was fall, and the gathering was at our house on Island Lake, and
the sauna was warming up as we watched Sandy open presents. We ate chili
and commenced to discuss stuff. Then some deer hunters came shouting
up the hill, and I ran to the door to see a huge billow of smoke and flame.

One of my friends (Stephanie) had the wherewithal to find the gas line
and disconnect it. Another (Cheryl) drove out to the main road to lead in
the fire trucks. The rest hosed down the house wall closest to the flames,
and I called 911. After a while, as the flames rose, I called again. The engines
and the volunteers arrived. The real firefighters sent us inside.

When they were done, the volunteer fireman in charge came in. He
said that the 911 operator had called him twice on the way, just to make
sure. The operator described me, the caller, as being "frantic, but cordial."

The phrase has ever since been a favorite of mine. "Frantic, but cordial"
is just so typical of so many of us. It is so real, and kind of Scandinavian, and
Garrison Keillor-like. Once, while waiting tables in a nice place, I served
a wine the way I was taught to serve it, with the testing and swirling and
all. The diner crooked his little finger, closed his eyes, and pronounced the
wine to be "sassy, but not impertinent." I wanted to laugh out loud.

Since then, I have heard wines described as many things: "casual,
but elegant," "self-righteous, yet not Republican," "mewling, yet bel-
licose," and I have always wanted to ceremoniously swish a swallow

through my teeth and proclaim the juice to be "frantic, but cordial."

I will probably never use the phrase with wine, but I will apply it to the Duluth School District's Music Task Force, a group formed to ask the board to clarify the intentions for music education in our public schools. It was composed of vocal, instrumental, and elementary music instructors; parents; and school board and central administration representatives. It was formed in response to years of cuts in personnel, increased student participation, and unclear expectations as to the scope and the quality and the quantity of performance and instruction provided. Most of the staff members in the music programs in our schools were hired during flusher times. There were district level coordinators and funds to repair instruments and to travel and to provide lessons. During these leaner years, the lessons are gone, there are sparse funds, and the questions have become fundamental, even foundational.

> *Music and all the arts are not in the headlines. They are not being tested and used to rank schools.*

"Do we do a great job for some children, or do we do a perfunctory job for all children?"

"Do we let all children discover their ability for creation, for leadership, for participation, for community, for the appreciation of something truly beautiful through music, or do we do so only for some children?" If the answer is "some" because we cannot afford to do so for all, then the question becomes, "Which ones?" How do we ethically decide which children get band, get orchestra, get choir, get to be musicians? How important is music in our schools in relation to all other things?

The task force gathered opinions and information. They knew that the function of a public school is to serve its community, and they needed to know what the community values. They frantically tried to do the right thing, and they cordially asked for direction.

These are frantic, strident times. Music and all the arts are not in the headlines. They are not being tested and used to rank schools. But they are a means by which we can measure whether a child can see his or her own unique gifts, or can filter reality through experience and come up with soul. Our school board will soon be asked to support with resources the top priorities of this group of dedicated and concerned individuals. This is another of those times when art will discover its value. Value, of course, not being synonymous with worth. The task force, educators, and students served know that art's worth is immeasurable. They are proud, yet not prideful; accomplished, yet confused; overburdened, yet resilient; realistic, yet fixed on stars; and of course they are frantic, but oh, so caring, and careful, and cordial to the core.

V. LEADING

I T SEEMED, ONCE, THAT GREAT LEADERS CAME to this earth with a purpose, armed with gifts from the creator, and were often led by voices the rest of us could never hear. Legendary leaders were given magic, or treasures, or really good looks, or all of the above in various proportions.

Leading today still requires exceptional skills, but the days of Hercules, John Wayne, and Wonder Woman have given way to the all-too-human realities of real people placed in real positions who are being asked to live up to superhuman expectations with dwindling resources—especially in schools.

Expectations of school leaders include those of the public, having seen movies and read books that feature the lone, maverick principal who sticks up for the lone, maverick teacher who really does care about the kids. Lone mavericks are out there, but in today's world of education, they are rare, and they are often not very successful.

Schools are incredibly complex systems that have become increasingly restrictive and resistant to change for many reasons. Many of those reasons protect students from danger and from the whims of the day. Leaders in schools need to be very aware of boundaries, but savvy enough to hear the voices of supporters and dissenters. Great leaders create a scope in which to act and produce real and lasting results.

School leaders today are finding more and more ways to be collaborative, to share decision making, rather than retain an authority that becomes crippling and ineffective over time.

Good school leaders are creating systems that function to consistently seek information and learn from the information gathered. Schools with good leaders have real and important discussions that include parents, staff, community members, and administrators, and they seek consensus before plans are made.

Exceptional school leaders almost disappear. They become servants who clear the way for the school to lead itself to constant improvement. Exceptional school leaders create the systems and then make certain that those systems will work well no matter who sits in the chair in the main office.

Challenges for leadership in schools are not lightening up. We will need more and more leaders who can pave the way, rather than be the way, as we face the next generation of schoolchildren. These leaders will come from our own ranks—of mere mortals who may or may not hear voices the rest of us can't hear.

There Was Only One John Wayne

Leaders and leadership weathered great changes as our nation and world emerged from the Industrial and entered the Information Age. Leadership and expectations of leaders have changed in schools, too.

THERE ARE SCHOLARS WHO SPEND their entire careers researching what works in school leadership. That small slice in the big pie of management and leadership studies is the total and complete focus of the professional lives of several individuals. Names like Marzano, Glickman, Fullan, Lezotte, Cuban, Lambert, and Elmore come immediately to my mind.

What's shocking about these researchers, to many of us, isn't that they thrive and inspire, it is that they agree on so many things! One of the main big items that so many of these folk seem to say over and over is that the old style, the authoritarian style, of leadership just plain doesn't work, and maybe it never did. They seem to pretty much agree that the stereotype of the principal, the one with the clicking heels of doom aimed at the classroom door, the John Wayne figure that takes a stand alone, the one with the closed office door of death, isn't very effective in providing the leadership we need now in schools.

Research in educational leadership seems to point, over and over again, toward the need to share common purpose and to capitalize on the strengths of many...

Of course, the lone rangers of legend are out there. The magnificent Marva Collins and other remarkable leaders came, saw, and transformed. But the reason legends exist is due to their singularity, not to the fact that they are the common experience. Therefore, to find what works in schools, researchers look at leadership behavior, not genetics. We can replicate behavior. We are not currently capable or willing to replicate DNA to produce effective principals.

Research in educational leadership seems to point, over and over again, toward the need to share common purpose and to capitalize on the strengths of many, not on the whims, notions, or even expertise of a few. Educational leadership scholars seem to agree that we need to expand to hear the voices and wisdom of many, even as we need to consolidate and focus on clear, identified, and important goals and purposes.

Harvard's Richard Elmore, in *Building a New Structure for School Leadership* (2000, 35-36), states, "Large scale improvement requires concerted action among people with different areas of expertise and a mutual respect that stems from an appreciation of the knowledge and skill requirements of different roles." Elmore's research recognizes that effective leadership requires respect for the knowledge and skills of individuals from various constituencies.

This week, I attended a site council meeting where parents, students, teachers, support staff, community members, and school administrators sat together and discussed issues for over two hours, exhibiting such admirable respect. I watched as problems were solved because those at the table listened and valued the knowledge and experience of those who would be affected by decisions made. The idea of mutual respect and of utilizing the strengths and wisdom of many to find solutions really just makes huge sense. Why limit ourselves to the understanding of one person, or one group of similar persons, to address the complexities of educating for this century, when together we can access and find more ideas and discover new, innovative, and responsive answers?

In addition to using the thinking of many, researchers seem also to agree on the importance of establishing common purpose in schools. Carl Glickman, in his book *Leadership for Learning: How to Help Teachers Succeed* (2002, 6), comments, "Successful schools stand in great contrast to mediocre and low-performing schools where faculty work apart from each other without common purpose, and with self-centered beliefs that they are doing the best they can."

Thriving schools use the wisdom of many to work together to achieve clear, common purposes as united systems. Schools that take the difficult steps of facing and breaking through the isolation of their talented, dedicated, and hardworking individual staff members can strive, as unified systems, toward increased student success. Bringing the best of what works to the table and studying together to attain new and important insights requires commitment to collaboration, trust, and mutual respect.

There's that respect thing again. Researcher Alan Blankstein, in his book *Failure Is Not an Option: Six Principles That Guide Student Achievement in High-Performing Schools* (2004, 59), states, "The relationships among adults in the school greatly influence the extent to which students in that school will succeed academically."

Mutual respect helps students learn better according to best practices research. From what I can see, mutual respect for diverse understandings only has beneficial possibilities. Schools that model these behaviors seem to thrive. Could the corollary be that those schools that do not seek input toward common purpose and do not exhibit mutual respect for the roles of others are not realizing potential benefits for students and staff? I would guess, at least, the research provides food for thought.

Does Anybody Else
Remember April Dancer?

Imagine schools that really do utilize the abundance that surrounds us.

IT USED TO BE THAT MY BEST thing was playing "Let's Pretend." Some would say that it still is.

As a girl, after turning off the light switch on the wall, I used to leap over the rug to my bed, holding my feet up high off the ground so that the invisible witch under the bed couldn't snap off my toes.

My favorite game in the world was played at my friend Gail's farm, when she pretended she was Emma Peel from *The Avengers,* and I pretended I was April Dancer, *The Girl from U.N.C.L.E.* We usually teamed up to rescue Mrs. Peel's absent husband from somewhere where there were countless ill-intended individuals who would foil our attempt. We hid from them behind hay wagons and grain bins. We took aim at them and threw dried things at them from the silo ladder. We rode her horses bareback in the ditches, and we always got away. We never rescued Mr. Peel. He would have most likely been anticlimactic anyway.

The point is, of course, that I am very experienced at complex and nuanced, high-level make-believe. Now that I have established my expertise at pretending, I would like to engage those skills and concentrate on schools.

So, let's pretend. But let's start with some facts.

According to the Coalition for Community Schools (n.d.), it's possible to create and maintain schools that are open early and close late seven days a week, all year long!

"Community schools" are schools that are designed to be "hubs" that "foster enduring relationships among educators, families, community volunteers, businesses, health and social services agencies, youth development organizations, and others committed to children.... partnerships of excellence" (2).

Community schools operate in public school buildings and are open to students and families and the community before and after school. The schools are oriented toward the community and include programs designed to expand horizons and build on school learning. These schools may have medical and dental help or mental health and family counseling services available on site. Some community schools are partnered with YMCAs and YWCAs, artists, college faculty and students, business people, and cross-generational groups. These places "crackle with excitement."

The ideas are endless.
The opportunities are endless.

So, let's pretend that our high schools decided to lean toward integrating some of the principles of community schools. Imagine how such places could be!

Parents, community members, social service agencies, and volunteers would plan together to maximize the use of our really outstanding high school facilities. Just think of our high schools, where our students could stay late for tutoring, enrichment, or both. They could stay late and learn how to catch a fish, sew a coat, or play bridge. Imagine a student taking advantage of dental hygiene as well as other health services on site. Community members would be able to use fitness facilities, career services, computers, and libraries. Together, generations could learn how to bake a perfect peach pie, be introduced to elements of interior design, or partake in the discussion of a great piece of literature. Summer, spring, winter, and fall, schools would offer continuous learning opportunities, as well as chances for communities to connect, share stories, and pass on skills and wisdom.

People would come to know one another, build trust, build friendships, and solve problems. The schools would become pivotal points in their corridors for all the citizens who surround them. They would be places where young parents could learn about raising infants without losing their marbles. They would be places where infants could receive checkups and attention from qualified volunteers. The schools could house day care and could host seminars regarding illness, wellness, and child development, with advice from mothers and fathers who had been down the same paths already.

Community schools could be sites for the donation of toys, clothing, children's furnishings, and books. The schools could be the jumping-off points for walks around the neighborhood with botanists, geologists, or historians, and collection points for water and air quality data, bird sightings, and community opinions. Plays and productions could feature folk from ages four to a hundred and four, and local businesses could provide informational talks during breakfasts. Field trip clubs could meet on Saturdays. Homework help could be provided every day. College classes and English as a Second Language classes could be made available on a regular basis for all generations. Food shelves could be stocked and attended by young people learning about service to community.

The ideas are endless. The opportunities are endless. Community schools, like the search for Emma Peel's husband, are not about a destination or a prize at the end. They are about the possibilities, the working together to achieve something great, and the imaginations of more than one. They are about the energy of dreamers. What a wonderful thing!

Making Hay While the Sun Shines

....

Schools and districts that take the time to create real and vital
improvement plans, based on important goals, set themselves up
for a great harvest of progress toward things that matter.

"The power to get people through the wilderness lay not
in the leader, but the vision." —William Bridges (1980)

IT IS DURING THESE BIG SKY DAYS, the occasional perfect summer
slice of heaven that we have gratefully basked in recently, when we can see
so clearly the need for a point of reference beyond the routine. We can sit
in the sunshine, look out at the glimmering lake, and make plans for the
long summer evenings. When we are done with our workdays, there is still
light and warmth and glorious opportunity. During these days of light, we
can see beyond the boxes we have built as protection, and we can choose
to revel in possibility. During these days, we dream, and through those
dreams, we can clarify and align our vision.

How appropriate, then, that this is the time when those schools with
brave leadership, established cultures of continuous improvement, and/or
strong site-based teams, engage in the process of refining vision, purpose,
and beliefs in order to determine their goals, based on solid information.
Then they systematically plan, accurately and realistically, how they will
achieve those goals. I have been and will be lucky enough to work with
some of those schools, and I have always been overwhelmed with the
incredible positive energy of groups made up of invested teachers, parents,
administrators, students, and community leaders.

When given the chance and processes to listen to one another,
when given good data and clear explanations, and when presented
with measurements that identify current conditions compared to what

is desired, these groups of invested stakeholders produce plans that are focused on students, not on the maintenance of institutions. When it is the vision, the idea of how we can be better, that is the focal point of the decision making, it is possible to move even the largest, most stable schools and districts toward a shared idea of education for the future.

Sometimes we make the mistake of managing instead of leading schools toward a shared vision. We do what it is we have too often done: We don't face what the data is telling us, and we lose the focus on kids as it fades into buildings. We lose the focus on learning as it gets confused with teaching and curriculum. We lose the focus on what's best for kids and watch it move to what's best for adults. We forget whom we serve because we can't remember what we wanted to be when we had our first vision of educating and parenting the next generation.

A good strategic plan is created every three to five years, and improvement plans based on strategic plans are revisited and revised annually. A good strategic plan is based on a strong mission and vision, and it defines clear goals. It does not micromanage how to achieve those goals, but it does monitor progress toward them. A good strategic plan tells us where we expect to be, not how to get there.

It has been said that any route will do when there is no destination in mind, that if you don't know where you are going, any road will get you there. I would venture to add that if you don't have a destination, no road you take will get you closer. Without revisiting a vision and planning a path toward lessening the space between where we are and where we want to be, schools will have wasted the opportunity on these clear, see-forever days of summer and will return in the fall to the cold, dark, and fog, and slog on down unclear paths toward no defined destination, and it will unfortunately feel like business as usual.

What a bummer. C'mon, it's summer; let's use the light.

Newbies and Not Paying Attention

···

Each new school year, leaders in buildings and districts face new expectations, alignments, and dances of power and control.

I AM SURROUNDED BY QUESTIONABLE LEADERSHIP, and I am being quite bad. I suppose this is a survival skill I have learned and earned over a long life of sitting in classrooms. I am currently writing this column as I sit at a table in a seminar at the Minnesota Department of Education in Roseville. I will look up and nod at the presenter on an intermittent basis in order to create the illusion that I am taking notes, but in truth, I am multitasking. I wanted to write these thoughts before I forgot them, so I am risking the possibility of someone else's profundity passing me by, but that's just how it goes sometimes. Sometimes we just don't get to know everything.

The questionable leadership I am feeling, hanging heavy in the air, starts at the state level and permeates all the way to the classrooms. I don't mean that I am questioning existing leadership. Instead, I am referring to the many new expectations, so many new programs and people, in so many new positions, in so many schools and districts this fall. I feel as if we are witnessing a giant ritualized ceremony, not unlike male herring gulls when they face off and stare each other down as they walk around in a spaced-off circle before they engage. The gulls size each other up—analyzing strengths and seeking weak spots and vulnerabilities—as they decide whether to fly together or fight one another.

On the state level, the questions setting leadership scrambling involve the flexibility and safe harbor emerging in the controversial No Child Left Behind Act, and the new opportunities for Minnesota teacher pay scales under the Quality Compensation for Teachers (Q-Comp) legislation.

At the district level, as I sit here far away misbehaving, Superintendent Keith Dixon is leading a full-day meeting with principals to begin to establish a mutual flight plan for working together this school year. I would imagine the new superintendents in Hermantown, Cloquet, and everywhere else will be holding similar sessions to figure out ways and means as well.

The Herring Gull Face–Off Dance is repeated and reflected with new principals and staff, and again in each classroom, as the school year swoops in upon us. The dance is not a new one, but the rules are changing, more each year, creating a sort of maelstrom around the dancers, jacking up the urgency of the initial interactions between the leadership and those who would be led.

The dance is changing because the role of leaders in schools has changed dramatically. The principals, superintendents, program administrators, and teachers that we remember would certainly not be guaranteed positions, let alone successes, in the schools starting this fall. Educational leaders are not successful in today's schools because they know so much, because they have been there so long, because they are strong and powerful (or loudest), or even because they work really, really hard. They are successful, from my point of view, because they can create and maintain and capitalize on the strengths of strategic relationships, and because they keep the focus always and only on the students.

On the wall, here in this wing of the Minnesota Department of Education building, are the portraits of all the former Minnesota Commissioners of Education. The trends I see in the faces on the wall include the fact that the first twenty or so, up until 1983, seem to be all white men of a certain age and that they lasted in office for years and years and years. As I look at the past few decades, I do see some women, and I cannot help but note that the time spent in office seems to be shrinking. I see faces of commissioners I remember, who attempted to ride the surf of politics and changes in public education, some more successfully than others. Staying in leadership in public education at all levels is becoming increasingly slippery and illusive, it seems.

And so, as we begin a new school year, again we see the hopeful and fearful and energizing and challenging initiations of leaders, roles, and expectations at all levels. The work has become increasingly complex, intricate, and overwhelming, and there are no signs that it will lighten up.

(Here, back at the seminar, I feel the presenter's eyes upon me. I am sensing scorn. I can't bear the pressure.)

Godspeed to newbies everywhere. So much depends on your skills and talents, instincts and intuition. Probably too much, but Godspeed anyway, as you take off in this new year.

Potshots, Dreamers, and
Hiring Superintendents

Every year, districts everywhere take turns hiring new superintendents.
The positions are pivotal, and whoever we choose will create the
policies and systems that can define a district for decades.

IT IS JUST SO MUCH EASIER TO TAKE POTSHOTS at people, or groups of people, than it is to solve a problem. It doesn't take much work to blame or criticize. Sometimes it takes a little effort to blame and criticize wittily or cleverly, but the amount of effort expended is nothing compared to the effort it takes to get the work done. As I have continued to become older, and older, and older, I see less and less value in sophomoric bashing of those who are in the trenches and more and more value in honoring the willingness of those who put in real time and real effort and even real money to muck about in the realities and to try to fully understand and deal with the complexities of an issue.

Schools are complex issues.

To lead a school system requires deep and ready understandings of layers upon layers, worlds upon worlds, of politics, bureaucracies, systems, traditions, histories, finances, rules and regulations, accountability requirements, personnel management, allocation, communities, communications, change theory, leadership theory, cultures, expectations, power structures, futures studies, buildings and maintenance, athletics, arts, curricula, instruction, special needs, teaching, learning, and kids. This is probably not an exhaustive list, even. But it is impressive anyway.

Every year, districts all over will be choosing new leadership. Some districts will ask the community to be involved in specifying expected requirements for prospective leaders. Other districts, perhaps, will have forums for public participation in the hiring processes. It's a good idea. It may cut down on the potshot factor a bit for the person eventually hired. However, whoever is hired as superintendent in any district goes in knowing that it is a lonely and responsible position, with not nearly the positional power one might expect. It is a position that carries incredible potential to affect generations of citizens, but it is also a position that is considered fair game to public and unchallenged criticism, no matter what method of decision making is used.

So, here is my input as to the candidates' qualities. In addition to clear and deep understanding of all that has been mentioned so far in this column, I would like first to request that all the new superintendents hired be dreamers. If we continue to solve problems in the same ways, we will just end up

> *We need brave, but wise, risk takers; outstanding communicators; and candidates who love children...*

with more of the same problems. We need leaders who can figure out new solutions. We need inspired leadership that can capitalize on the strengths of our communities and the skills of our educators and bring us to new levels of success. Perhaps this will mean rethinking the system, but better that than the continued unreasonable strain on the current structure.

Second, we need leadership that the school boards will agree to respect and utilize. We need a clear set of expectations for the office, from the school boards, that delineates who makes what decisions, categorically. We need leadership that honors those expectations, even under pressure.

Third, we need ethical and responsible leadership from a team that includes central office and school board members. Therefore, we need an inspired and inspiring team player as leader.

In addition, we need brave, but wise, risk takers; outstanding communicators; and candidates who absolutely love children always, always, always.

We have been lucky in this region to have had leaders who exhibit all of these qualities and more, and we are the less for their loss. We have had leaders who have come into office with their own agendas, or lacking skills, and left us the worse after their departure. During these times, we cannot afford to bring in leadership that proposes simple answers to complex questions. We cannot afford to bring in leadership that spends huge amounts of time and energy in admiring and glorifying problems and little time or energy in solving them. We cannot afford to bring in leadership that blames others for situations and proposes no means of solution. We cannot afford to continue down the same path, when we can see that the path cannot continue. We can't afford to bring in leadership that is OK with the system's failure to respond to the needs of all learners. We can't afford to go backwards.

Leaders of school districts, be they superintendents or school board members, ultimately should be willing to muck about in the realities of districts and politics. They need to be willing to do the work and get dirty, take the potshots, put in the time it takes to attempt to solve the problems, and hang on to a vision of fair and responsible public education for all. They need to take on increasingly complex tasks, under increasingly sensational criticism. We need leaders who agonizingly know what they are up against, and who are willing to do the hard tasks anyway.

Let's just hope there are some very good ones out there, eager to roll up their sleeves, put on their armor, and go to work for us.

The Forever Conversation

*How do we stop talking about making changes in schools
and start making changes in schools?*

I FEEL AS THOUGH I HAVE BEEN PART of the same discussion forever. I feel as though I was born listening to all sorts of stakeholders talk about how schools should change, and I am afraid I will die sitting in a meeting where people are discussing how schools should change. I am not saying that schools haven't changed at all in my very long lifetime; we have. We have infused huge technologies, taken on incredible challenges, and kept students in school to graduate at rates that would have made my grandparents giggle with delight. We have made significant strides with social challenges that were too daunting to face even a generation ago. We have not grown

> *We have made significant strides with social challenges that were too daunting to face even a generation ago.*

any moss on our underbellies. Yet last week, I sat in another meeting and listened to debate over cuts in district staff once again, without any discussion about change of structure and design based on what we now know about schools, learning, teaching, and leading.

Drs. Dwight Allen and William Cosby, Jr. (yes, that Bill Cosby), recently published a book, *American Schools: The 100 Billion Dollar Challenge* (2000), which challenged the American public educational system to revamp. The authors proposed the development of a system of experimental schools under the administration of a new national organization—The National Experimental School Administration (NESA). NESA would provide communication, expectations, funding, and development in order that schools, located in every state, representing all types of delivery, would try researched best practices in teacher development, pre-service training programs, technology (including computers at home for every child and teacher), year-round and extended-day schooling, alternative schools, and accountability.

What we know about how children learn is increasing exponentially each year, yet instituting change in our schools is slow and cumbersome. Allen and Cosby advocate "dot-com" leadership for education. "Dot-com leadership implies vision, risk taking, caring, sharing, and enormous energy" (8). I have seen all of those attributes in school leaders everywhere around the Northland. So, I just think we need to start shaking things up a bit, and I would like to propose a place to start.

According to *Breaking Ranks* (2004), a groundbreaking study completed by the National Association of Secondary School Principals, a few factors separate schools that are extremely successful from schools that are not. One of the most important of those factors is the capacity to provide connection. Schools where all students have real relationships, with teachers or other students, provide a reason to come to school. Connection could involve extracurricular offerings, sports, small classes, advisor/advisee relationships, etc. We provide many opportunities for connection in our schools in this region. Yet, we all know students who do not take advantage of those opportunities. Students without connections are in our schools—at least for a while. They are the most at-risk group for leaving our system before they reach graduation.

I think we can start there. We can explore possibilities for each student in our public schools to have reasons to go to school and to have someone notice if he or she is no longer around, someone to whom it matters.

Connection also happens when schools feel smaller and are organized in different ways for different kids. According to Allen and Cosby, "Alternative schools should be encouraged and funded—but not as a disguised way of avoiding diversity or further segregating our kids and leaving behind the disadvantaged kids with no one to speak for them. Many alternatives can be developed within existing structures and facilities—schools within schools" (151). The authors go on to tell us that, by strategically developing alternatives, we are taking steps to provide the choices that encourage students to stay connected with school within the current system.

The idea of creating smaller learning communities that provide for connection for all kinds of kids is becoming reality in places all across this nation. According to a recent study, "A growing number of school districts around the country are using small school development as a central strategy for improving high schools and overhauling the way the district itself does business. Driven by an increasing sense of urgency and frustration with reforms that fail to fundamentally change the quality of instruction or the nature of student-teacher relationships, they are transforming large, under-performing high schools into 'education complexes' made up of multiple autonomous small schools under one roof" (Allen and Steinberg 2004, 1).

So, this could be a place to start. The idea of smaller schools within large high schools, developed strategically to build upon the strengths and interests of small groups of enrollees, could create the type of change we have been talking about. At least it should be part of the long and never ending conversation, from my point of view.

Relationships, Responsiveness, and Keeping It Real

....

Site councils are decision-making leadership groups in schools.
They are composed of faculty, support staff, parents, students (sometimes),
administrators, and community members. They keep the focus of schools
in line with the values and priorities of the communities they serve.

HERE'S WHAT I HAVE COME TO UNDERSTAND and believe. I believe that private schools, parochial schools, and even charter schools create their missions before they are founded. For instance, some private schools are formed to prepare students for college. Some are formed to prepare students for Ivy League colleges. Others specialize for students with physical disabilities, or they are designed to prepare students for high-ranking military positions. The reasons to form private schools are numerous and, well, private.

Parochial schools are formed to provide students with an education that includes the tenets of the faith of the designers and to provide opportunities for worship in school.

Charter schools are formed to serve a niche population within the public realm. Charters are granted to schools that wish to provide alternative delivery of instruction or a specific focus that forms a basis for their design.

Charter, parochial, and private and proprietary schools first choose their missions. The mission of these institutions attracts and creates a community that supports the institution.

The opposite is true of public schools. Public schools are placed in a community, and the community served forms each school's mission. The school itself is a public servant, responsible and responsive to the physical community surrounding it, and reliant on the interaction and satisfaction of the people it serves.

During the past two weeks, I have worked with two school communities through representative leadership teams called "site councils." Site councils are remarkable, living, breathing, vibrant organisms, and I had the privilege of facilitating an established, effective council from Duluth's Central High School and a newly re-forming group from Piedmont Elementary.

Good, strong site councils are composed of voluntary members who represent the community. They provide a forum for all voices to be heard. Good, strong site councils make real decisions, debate policy, and close the communication loop between stakeholders and public servants. Good, strong site councils form the mission and set the goals for the schools.

It's a beautiful thing to watch parents, community members, and staff listen to one another.

I watched two sets of volunteers in the past several days. These individuals gave their time and energy to sit and learn and deliberate together for eight to ten hours at a time. These people gave up vacation days, family time, and donated their energy and expertise to the schools in their communities. At Piedmont, there were eighteen individuals, and at Central, there were twenty-four.

Each group began by learning together and looking at the gaps between what the community and staff want to happen and what is actually happening in the schools. Each group finished by determining focus and direction for the year ahead.

It's a beautiful thing to watch parents, community members, and staff listen to one another. It's remarkable to see these teams react to the data presented, the research presented, and this year, to the vision of a new superintendent who came to speak and answer questions in each session. It is a wondrous thing to watch the trust build between parent and administrator, teachers and community, support staff and parents, and every link in between.

It is a rewarding and happy thing to see the voices grow stronger as faith in the process is established and institutionalized.

And yet, the process always comes back to the individuals involved. When I think of site council successes, I see faces. I see Portia, a community member from Central, who has volunteered countless hundreds of hours because she believes. I see her small fist in the air, blocking a consensus, because on a site council, it only takes one fist, any fist, to force us all to reconsider. I also see a goal, rewritten because of her block, as a stronger, better, more inclusive, and more responsive goal. Each year she is there, regal, responsible, and real, making a real difference.

This year, I saw a new group of parents and community members from Piedmont as they struggled to digest achievement data, and I watched them become proficient at tossing around the acronyms that rule our world (NCLB, AYP, MCA, IDEA, FY, GLC, SD) and the concepts of intersecting data points and multiple measures. I watched the new council at Piedmont create its first set of annual goals.

The idea of public education is new, relatively, to this world. We are learning every day how to make it work. Providing the means by which we can hear one another is keeping our schools true to the purpose for which they were created. The relationship between the community and the public school is what keeps the school alive. Indeed, it is the only reason for the existence of the institution, and unless that relationship is honored and protected, the institution will no longer have a purpose that matters in the end to anyone at all. We need one another, and that's a beautiful thing, indeed!

Shoes and Still Waters

On Sunday, May 16, 2004, at 4:30 in the morning, the Minnesota State Legislature voted not to confirm the appointment of Cheri Pierson Yecke as the State Commissioner of Education. Dr. Yecke was appointed to the position by Governor Tim Pawlenty and took the helm of the agency when he took the helm of the state. While under her leadership, the state's standards for schools were repealed, and new sets of standards were developed.

THERE IS A STORY, OFTEN TOLD, of a Rip Van Winkle–type character who fell asleep in the hills about forty or fifty years ago. For some reason, he woke recently and wandered into the heart of the city he had slumbered beside. Dazed, confused, afraid, and shy, he found he did not know how to function. He barely recognized his own hometown. There were hotels and restaurants and tourists where he used to work. There was traffic and a weird birdcall thing going on downtown. He had no plastic to pay for anything, and he could find no real person on the other end of phone calls. He wandered lost and sad and frantic, and then he stumbled into his very own alma mater high school. He walked in the door. The bell rang, and he knew just what to do. He knew where to go and how to perform, and he recognized the lessons.

This story can be either reinforcing or terrifying, depending on your point of view. The fact that schools pretty much stay the same while the rest of the world drastically alters could be good, or could be scary, depending on what is valued in the argument. Cheri Pierson Yecke entered office with what was perceived to be a mandate to overthrow an enacted reform, commonly known as the Profile of Learning. She and her supporters were successful. Then she created committees that wrote new standards that identified what students need to be taught. The new sets of standards were the replacement

188 JULES ON SCHOOLS

sets for standards written by committees a few years before. Dr. Yecke was a very hard worker, tireless and smart, and she needed to be. She was filling a position that has become an incredibly difficult assignment. The tenures of the past several Commissioners of Education have been relatively short and abundant with controversy.

The pattern kind of feels familiar. The new Commissioner comes in and goes to work unraveling the work of the previous office holders, and weaving something else. The result of repeated attempts to establish policy and procedures through political processes is not easily measured. It appears, however, that what is referred to as the "instructional core" remains calm and unruffled and unchanged. What happens between the teacher and the student, the "core" of what we do, seems untouched by politics and policy and pundits and potshots and passage of time.

Education theorist Larry Cuban (1993) compared school reform to the ruffled waters of a big lake in a storm. The wind howls, ships are tossed, and people yell and scream. Some flee, and it is tumultuous to say the least. Yet, deep below the surface, down where the fish really live and swim in schools, it is calm and smooth and sweet and still.

Bringing reform efforts to the classroom where they actually could affect the children may never happen due to storming and surging of standards on the surface. Legislative actions, board policy, commissioner after commissioner's agendas, state and federal mandates, and funding streams fight and collide with great force year after year.

Those at the surface work hard and do their jobs. We need individual leaders who believe and are willing to struggle to uphold their beliefs. But the place where reform becomes real is in the relationship between the teacher and the students. I have seen teachers who care deeply, who protect children from the colliding ideologies of school governance, and who institute giant changes in practice and in beliefs when given the chance to examine their own practices in light of researched, justified new best practices. I have seen children benefit from classrooms where reform, based on real data and real analysis, is cautiously and respectfully implemented.

Way down below the surface, schools and classrooms move slowly as they go about their business. They always will. Schools have seen too many storms at the surface and are pretty leery about swimming up to check things out. Besides, there's much to attend to every single day, down below.

A wonderful office manager at the elementary school that most of my children attended once told me that it's a good, good day when everybody goes home with their own shoes.

I don't want to wake up in forty years and see that education has done only box steps, that we have continued to weave and unravel in equal measures over and over again, that the bell rings and I know exactly what to do. We do so need to stop storming relentlessly at the surface, changing policy, changing direction, whirling about and about. We do so need to focus that amazing talent and energy and strength, please, on the places where it can matter most—on the children, on the teachers, on principals, and on finding the right and best ways to teach and learn and hang on to our own shoes.

References

Allen, Dwight W., and William H. Cosby, Jr. 2000. *American schools: The 100 billion dollar challenge.* New York: iPublish/Time Warner.

Allen, L., and A. Steinberg. 2004. *Big buildings, small schools: Using a small schools strategy for high school reform.* http://www.jff.org/jff/PDFDocuments/smallschools.pdf (accessed May 25, 2005).

Blankstein, Alan M. 2004. *Failure is not an option: Six principles that guide student achievement in high-performing schools.* Thousand Oaks, CA: Corwin Press.

Bridges, William. 1980. *Transitions: Making sense of life's changes.* Reading, MA: Addison-Wesley.

Caine, Renate N., and Geoffrey Caine. 1997. *Unleashing the power of perceptual change: The potential of brain-based teaching.* Alexandria, VA: Association for Supervision and Curriculum Development.

Citizens League Report on Higher Education in Minnesota. 2004. *Trouble on the Horizon: Growing Demands and Competition, Limited Resources, and Changing Demographics in Higher Education.* http://www.citizensleague.net

Coalition for Community Schools. n.d. *Community schools: Partnerships for excellence.* Washington, D.C: Institute for Educational Leadership. http://www.communityschools.org/partnerships.html

Cuban, Larry. 1993. *How teachers taught: Constancy and change in American classrooms 1880-1990.* 2nd ed. New York: Teachers College Press.

Elmore, Richard F. 2000. *Building a new structure for school leadership.* Washington, DC: Albert Shanker Institute.

Gilbert, Thomas F. 1996. *Human competence: Engineering worthy performance.* Tribute edition. Washington, DC: International Society for Performance Improvement.

Glickman, Carl D. 2002. *Leadership for learning: How to help teachers succeed.* Alexandria, VA: Association for Supervision and Curriculum Development.

Loewen, James W. 1996. *Lies my teacher told me: Everything your American history textbook got wrong.* New York: Simon & Schuster.

National Association of Secondary School Principals. 2004. *Breaking ranks II: Strategies for leading high school reform.* Reston, VA: National Association of Secondary School Principals.

Pajak, Edward. 2003. *Honoring diverse teaching styles: A guide for supervisors.* Alexandria, VA: Association for Supervision and Curriculum Development.

Schlechty, Phillip C. 2002. *Working on the work: An action plan for teachers, principals, and superintendents.* San Francisco: Jossey-Bass.

Stiggins, Richard J. 2005. Looking at assessment through new eyes. Keynote address, Minnesota Association for Supervision and Curriculum Development Winter Conference, Minnetonka, MN.

Stiggins, Richard J., J. A. Arter, J. Chappuis, and S. Chappuis. 2004. *Classroom assessment for student learning: Doing it right—using it well.* Portland, OR: Assessment Training Institute.

Wiggins, Grant P. 1998. *Educative assessment: Designing assessments to inform and improve student performance.* San Francisco: Jossey-Bass.

Index

M

N

P

T